M000158860

FORTIS

The Origin of Things

Sketches, Models, Prototypes

Thimo te Duits

With contributions by:
Philip van Daalen
Lesley Hoskins
Peter van Kester
Henrik Most
Paolo Palma
Jane Pavitt
Michael Siebenbrodt
Johan Soetens
Penny Sparke
Pauline Terreehorst
Gareth Williams
Peter Zwaal

Museum Boijmans Van Beuningen Rotterdam
NAi Publishers Rotterdam

About the Things

In the last few years within the profession of industrial design there has been increasing attention on the story behind the object, in which sketches, design drawings, models and prototypes play a prominent role. They make possible a reconstruction of the interesting history of their origin. Above all they make visible the designer's contribution, which is often very different to what one might expect. The role played by technology and the demands of the market are also elucidated. By focusing on these aspects within the museum context design is made more real – less form and more content.

Since the establishment of the Industrial Design department in 1982, scores of prototypes have found their way into the collection. It has even availed itself of entire archives of a number of notable Dutch designers. Within the last few years the collecting of prototypes has become an express remit. A number of highpoints from *The Origin of Things*, such as the vases by Frank Lloyd Wright, have only recently been acquired.

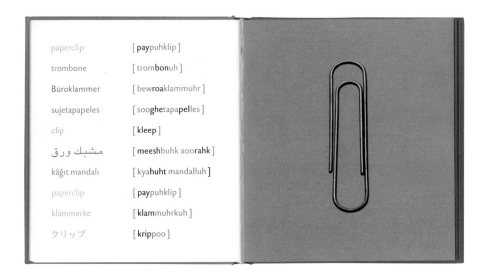

paperclip	[**pay**puhklip]
trombone	[trom**bon**uh]
Büroklammer	[**bew**roaklammuhr]
sujetapapeles	[soo**ghe**tapapelles]
clip	[kleep]
مشبك ورق	[**meesh**buhk aoorahk]
kâğıt mandalı	[**kya**huht mandalluh]
paperclip	[**pay**puhklip]
klammerke	[**klam**muhrkuh]
クリップ	[**krip**poo]

Amongst the many publications produced by the museum's relatively new Industrial Design department, one stands out in every regard as an oddity, the *Things* catalogue from 1998. It is actually nothing more than a picture book for children. Around seventy-five illustrations of objects give a wonderful glimpse of the collection's great variety. This special book also functions as a multilingual dictionary. Each picture is accompanied by its name in ten (!) languages, making the book into a multicultural children's primer.

Things was the first in a series of books in which the museum has sought to make

Philippe Starck, tooth-brush *Fluocaril*, 1989, plastics, length 19.5 cm

design accessible in a surprising manner. *The Origin of Things* is its successor. It is written for a broad public; accessible, surprising and informative.

To mark the re-opening of the museum, we have decided to show the state of play of the collecting of prototypes. The most remarkable products have been selected and supplemented with a few that provide the ideal context for our own collection. How fantastic would it be to exhibit Richard Buckminster Fuller's Dymaxion Car alongside the visionary plaster models of Theodor Bogler's Kombinationsteekanne? How much richer would our collection of Olivetti office machines be if we had also been able to acquire Mario Bellini's foam models?

For a few weeks we have turned this dream image of the ideal collection into a reality, and documented it for posterity in this publication. We are enormously indebted to our many colleagues at home and abroad who have helped to locate objects and documentation, who have written essays for this publication, and who have agreed to lend extremely fragile pieces. Our thanks are also due to the designers who have granted us a peek into their own practice.

Interest in design is growing steadily. The fact that a famous designer has played a part in the birth of a more beautiful – and we hope also a better – product is for many people a good reason to reach deeper into their pockets.

Design objects are objects of desire. In the novel *Les Choses – Things* – by Georges Perec, the desire for products occupies the foreground. The main protagonists – a young married couple – have developed an almost maniacal desire for the best and most beautiful, a desire that alas remains unattainable. They represent the growing drive for consumption after the Second World War. The 1950s also marked a period of transition: the establishment of industrial design as an independent discipline in the Netherlands. In the 1930s America had led the way with designers such as Norman Bel Geddes, Henry Dreyfuss and Raymond Loewy. Europe adopted the American model only later.

It is not for nothing that we mention the well-known French writer Perec here. His masterpiece, *La Vie, Mode d' Emploie – Life, a User's Manual –*, was an important inspiration for this catalogue. His huge novel presents itself as a riddle that slowly unravels itself. The hook for the story is formed by a Parisian apartment block that yields up its secrets through the reconstruction of the histories of its inhabitants and their relationships with each other. Puzzles also play a mysterious leading role in this work. The making of jigsaw puzzles, the assembling

Konstantin Grcic/Authentics, tub *Two Hands*, 1995, plastics, Ø 59 cm

The average housewife recognises her desires firstly in their fulfilment.

Wim Gilles, 1957

of the pieces and the invisible mending of the joints appears repeatedly throughout the novel. The book is actually an ode to reconstruction.

The Origin of Things is an anthology of reconstructions. Together the stories of thirty-three products provide an image of the changes within the discipline of industrial design. Highlights from the history of design and remarkable design strategies are included to show how, over the years, the work of artist-designers and engineers has been taken over by industrial designers. These specialists chart production processes and are better positioned than anyone else to bring about improvements to all manner of things. In addition this book also examines the recent counter-movement of young designers who have taken up the position of artists.

A number of the stories concern products such as the paperclip and the bottle for Odol mouthwash, which have remained unaltered for years – sometimes for even more than a century – demonstrating their superior form and function. The quest to produce furniture from a single piece of material, now ongoing for more than seventy years, is another remarkable story. Verner Panton's designs for Herman Miller and Thonet follow seamlessly from Gerrit Rietveld' various designs for his Zigzag chair and their history finds a contemporary successor in the folded tables by Konstantin Grcic.

Many products have been paired with each other to produce surprising and enlightening confrontations and to facilitate fascinating comparisons: fashion, graphic design, cutlery, chairs, vases, typewriters, cars, bottles and domestic appliances. The ability to show, step-by-step, how a product came into being was an important and practical consideration in the definitive selection of the objects. They include a range of prototypes with a pronounced visionary or manifesto-like character, ending with the newest of the new. So, Rem Koolhaas invariably views his architecture as a form of prototype. His shop in New York for the clothing company Prada has been consciously designed so that the building is never complete and will remain constantly in a state of flux. The very newest objects to be included in this book are still unfinished at the time of going to press. Dick van Hoff's kitchen appliances are still in development and have come about in response to a request from the museum to reflect upon the other items included in *The Origin of Things*.

We have expressly chosen to represent each designer with just a single story. However, we have made an exception for Wim Gilles, an industrial designer of the first order. Since 1980 Museum Boijmans Van Beuningen has administered his archive. His DRU kettle and fold-up scooter are such fantastic products that to choose between them proved impossible. During the preparation of this project Gilles unexpectedly died. We dedicate both the exhibition and this book to his memory.

Chris Dercon, Artistic Director
Hugo Bongers, Financial Director

Thimo te Duits, Curator of Design

Contents

There is a clear difference between the amateur camera by industrial designer Raymon Loewy and the engineer's style of Leica for a professional camera.

Raymond Loewy/Purma Cameras Ltd, *Purma Special*, 1937, bakelite, height 7.5 cm

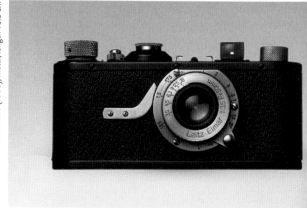

Oskar Barnak/Ernst Leitz AG, *Leica 1A*, 1914-1936 (1930), metal, length 13.3 cm

A designer must have a radar on his head

Wim Gilles was the Netherlands' first industrial designer. He formed a bridge between two periods and two worlds. Shortly after the Second World War he introduced a theoretical approach to the design profession in the Netherlands. After a period in which artists had developed products through a process of trial and error, he introduced new American ideas that were based on a systematic approach.

Gilles opted for a position that had hitherto been occupied by engineers. He laid a solid basis for the profession of industrial design in the Netherlands, not only as a designer, but also as the director of, amongst others, the Academy for Industrial Design in Eindhoven. In November 2002 Gilles gave an interview that turned into a three-hour-long masterclass. By way of introduction to *The Origin of Things* there follows a selection from that interview. A few weeks after the interview Wim Gilles died.

Henry Dreyfuss/The American Thermosbottle Co., *Thermos flask*, 1935, plastics, glass and aluminium, height 14.7 cm

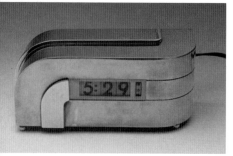

Kem Weber/Lawson Time Inc., *The Zephyr clock*, 1934, copper, height 9 cm

Who was Wim Gilles?

Gilles was an exceptionally devoted teacher. I got to know him when I was teaching at the Technical University in Delft. But above all he was an extremely special designer, a trailblazer. Gilles was a real doer, a practical man. He was one of the founders of the Association of Dutch Industrial Designers (KIO) in 1952. The KIO was of great importance in the professionalisation of design. Gilles led the way. After a few years a group of culturally committed designers split from the organisation. Gilles wanted nothing to do with this sort of designer, who in his eyes were stylists who make things look pretty. Gilles was no stylist. The first American industrial designers were the stylists, just think of Loewy who came out of the fashion world, or Henry Dreyfuss. Somebody who was really a great example for Gilles was, of course, Buckminster Fuller. He brought engineering and aesthetics together.

You cannot speak of style or aesthetics with Gilles. He tried to get as far away as possible from aesthetics. Gilles came out of a generation of engineer-designers, he was a mechanical engineer. He was technically well versed. Designers are a mixture of different disciplines. They always look further than their own field. That is why they are so good at consumer products. They have a better feel for what the market wants than manufacturers, who are imprisoned in their own ideas. When a designer takes something on it is always more ingenious, and often more beautiful. They apply knowledge from other areas, they look to other disciplines. That's how you get new ideas. A designer must have a radar on his head.

Industrial design can no longer be practiced by just a single person. Independence is almost impossible. The industrial designer is a good head of a team. He is the leader or policy former of a project. Industrial design is not about the final furlong, it is about the process. The three groups – design, marketing and technology – must be fused into a whole. If you've got that under control, you can break new ground.

Thimo te Duits, interview with Wim Crouwel, January 2003

Interview Wim Gilles
2002

What was the set up for industrial design shortly after the Second World War?

Of course, in the beginning people didn't know what industrial design was. At first I didn't realise that I myself was an industrial designer at all. Jan Samson, my boss, had an edition of *Art & Industry*, a very small English magazine. That must have been in 1947 or 1948. It was about industrial design. It seemed that I was an industrial designer after all.
In the beginning there was a large demand for information in books and magazines. The Institute for Industrial Design published a series of small brochures. I wrote the section aimed at manufacturers as part of the methodology that we were beginning to develop. At first we simply tried things out. You went to your drawing board and simply began, but of course that was completely inefficient. Slowly you picked up tips on how to do it systematically. Eventually you understood that you shouldn't begin with design. First you had to analyse, to know what the problem was. The entire methodology was formed gradually.

But didn't you pick up the craft from others, architects for example?

No, we industrial designers were concerned with the business of functional analysis and so on much earlier than the architects. They did it much later. But in practice you didn't employ a systematic approach to design anywhere near all the time. I discovered in my own practice that in some cases such research was just a load of codswallop. Nine out of ten times you worked back to front. That was how you reached the solution. And what was the problem again? If you teach, to make it learnable – didactic – of course you can't do without methodology. Without it, you just get nonsense! The value of a systematic working method is for the most part educational and not so much practical.

How did you design then, at the time?

Do you know the term heuristics? In science you pose a hypothesis, and it is true as long as you cannot prove that it isn't (this is Karl Popper's theory.) Science is therefore a process of verification. That is a bit of traditional scientific thinking, to draw a conclusion on the basis of establishing a few facts, and to deduce from all the facts that there appears to be a general rule. We call that a law. Heuristics is

Although industrial design had already been practiced for as long as factory production had existed, people came to realise only for the first time after the Second World War, and initially very reluctantly, that a specialist, such as an architect, could also be of use in the manufacture of a coffee grinder or a vacuum cleaner.

Product: the aim

On this point every designer will give you the same answer – that the material, the construction to be employed, the required working method, the appropriate finish and the colour, is less important than the product itself … that it is merely one of the means to make that product fulfil the continually changing criteria of:

1. function – appropriateness for use
2. rationale – appropriateness for manufacture
3. desirability – appropriateness for the market.

It is, in fact, always the product that the designer must keep in mind and upon which he must reflect, and he must consider the material and the choice of materials in that light.

Wim Gilles, *Polytechnisch tijdschrift*, October 1955

based on known pieces of information. If you're a carpenter, it is known (by passed down information) that you don't hold a nail by its point, bur rather with the point downwards. That has never been shown scientifically. You just do it like that. You'll discover if it doesn't work. That is heuristics, an ancient Greek way of doing things that has been denied by science for centuries. You just do something. It's a matter of trial and error. There is therefore a hueristic school and I belong to that school.

How does that express itself in practice?

What we do is a sort of glorified trial and error. If you find a way of doing something that enables you to do it more quickly, then it's cheaper than when you just fiddle about for a year. You have to see it. If you've learned to work according to the heuristic method, then you can do a lot of useful work and you don't waste any energy. You become very handy at it.

So, you are suggesting that you believe in working within a particular field in order to acquire particular knowledge and experience with which you can progress.

Yes, by definition I would say, because as a designer you are not able to do everything. I think that it's nonsense to design products without knowing anything about it. I think that that is not possible. That is kidding yourself. When I began I had absolutely no background, except for a little bit of mechanical engineering, road building and hydraulics. The poor aesthetic that I began to perpetuate came entirely from my in-depth knowledge of typefaces. At the beginning of my career I drew book titles and they had to be Bodoni-like. And I really immersed myself in that. Much later I generalised that in other things. You start with a very small area and then you see what can be applied to other areas and combine it with the whole heuristics.

And does that result in an applicable system for everyone?

Yes, it is therefore actually a question of common sense, shrewdness, skill, and of course you can stick all sorts of lovely scientific labels on it, but it has sod-all to do with science.
Another thing of great importance, and which for centuries has been in the bad books, is imagination. Plato considered that it bordered on madness. And in England for a long time it was seen as mere

Product Analysis

The conception of the product

Sometimes Dutch industry seems to forget that the factory, with its increasingly specialised personnel, its increasingly ingenious and efficient machines, exists only by the grace of its products. If these are not correctly conceived, then all the effort spent on the means of productions is in vain. Seen in this light, the conception of the final product is one of the most essential occupations.

Trial and error

The usual state of affairs is that 'the market' requires a new product that can be described in two words. The draughtsman or design engineer is obliged to prepare the drawings within two months or less, so that, following the directorate's approval, a prototype can be exhibited to the public at the very next spring or autumn fair. The 'trade-that-knows-its-market' accepts or rejects, whereupon the product, without modification, is let loose on the consumers.

The real successes, carried out in this manner, are few. Mostly the procedure must be repeated one or more times, so that you can make use of market experience.

Questions and answers

One of the fundamental tenets of organised industrial design is that a product must provide the answer to a question. It is self-evident that one cannot formulate an answer to a question that has not yet been posed. Awareness of the demand must therefore be the first step in the direction of the conception of the product. This is far more important than producing a sketch, probably more difficult too, and the result may be that the sketch is also arrived at less easily, but nonetheless with a greater chance of market success.

Two aids

There are two aids known, which enable us to gauge the demand for a product. The oldest and best known is market research, which is concerned with the extent and the situation of the demand.

Recently another aid has been developed, which has become known as 'product analysis'.

The aim of product analysis

The deduction and formulation of established and accurate guidelines for the conception of a product.

Wim Gilles, *Industriële vormgeving, de productanalyse*, 1957

fancy. That's not allowed, that is dirty. In the *Critique of Pure Reason*, Immanuel Kant followed for the first time other philosophers such as Socrates, who did find imagination interesting.

Imagination is an extremely handy means of testing if something works. It is a word that every designer uses, but actually never realises it: what if? What if I do this, what happens then? Drawing conclusions in your mind and seeing them before you. I can design sitting in my car. In principle I don't need a drawing board, I don't need paper or a computer programme. As a designer I can imagine anything. I can manipulate things in my mind. There are people who cannot do that. Well, they are better off not being designers.

What are the characteristics of industrial design?

Industrial design is not something that someone does. Industrial design happens. If all designers no longer existed, things would still be designed. Factories continue to manufacture. More than one person takes part in designing. In my work, the 'scooterette' is actually a complete exception. I was simply tinkering about by myself in the cellar of my house in Bergeijk. Few others had anything to do with it. Certainly no manufacturer, because I knew what they could and could not make. Industrial design doesn't grow on trees. There's something more to it, and at that time we had great difficulty in reaching that insight. Making a prototype is not industrial design. Reproduction is industrial design. Actually the prototype is of no importance.

Why do you make prototypes then?

To begin with you make something to show that it is possible, such as the small scooter, for example. It's the same if you design a house. You only know if it's good if you can live in it. With industrial design its already reckoned in that ten million of them will be made. If you make a hundred thousand it's another matter.

How were you received as an industrial designer by DRU in the beginning?

Of course DRU was a very traditional company, it was still in the nineteenth century. The then director, Ingen Housz, was a very clever man. I learned a lot from him. As soon as I arrived at DRU I had to go and see him in his office. He said, "You have to know this company from inside and out. That is of great importance for your work. You must

The implementation of product analysis

I

Assemble all those products with which the new product will have to compete.

II

Study the aforementioned products in depth, for which the following aspects are important:

1　Date of design

2　Functional principle

3　Fulfilment of regulations (e.g. standardisation)

4　Functional requirements (e.g. required energy)

5　Safety

6　Functional capabilities and limitations (e.g. capacity)

7　Hygienic characteristics

8　Maintenance and servicing possibilities

9　Life span

10　Uses and limitations

11　Extent of protection of rights (e.g. patents)

12　Choice of materials

13　Construction

14　Packaging

15　Storage possibilities and limitations

16　Existing sales pitch

17　Means of distribution

18　Price and value

19　Trade discounts

20　Approximate volume of sales

21　Identity of the purchaser

22　Identity of the user

23　Visual impression

24　Tangible impression

III

Collate the positive and negative aspects of the products studied, and compare them in order to draw conclusions with which to formulate guidelines for the new product, which should possess as many of the positive characteristics as possible and as few of the negative ones as possible.

Wim Gilles, *Industriële vormgeving, de productanalyse*, 1957

not be distracted by what other people say, what they want, what they want you to do. It is my order that you don't touch a drawing board or pencil for the first two months. Get to know every department. Refuse all the other work. If you don't do that now, you will never do it." And that is true. Two months later I was familiar with everything and knew how it worked.

How important was the influence of the sales department in the development of products at the time?

The salespeople always played very safe. During my study trip to America I learned how you should really do it. I had made a suggestion about how to handle the product development at DRU. You must have someone as a mediator between the designer and the salespeople, who is head of the product planning department. I learned that at General Electrics. This was a mechanism to set it in the right track.

And how important and influential is the client?

Just as important as the designer.
A designer must make it clear to his client:
1 that he considers the company for which he works as his company;
2 that such a designer considers himself almost the replacement for the director;
3 that he can expect to have support from the top;
4 that what he does is the best that he can do.

In what kind of environment did you end up at DRU?

At the beginning the designers were the model makers, and they were 'artisans'. They made wood shavings. They were half sculptors. They made everything out of clay. They never made drawings. The mould maker didn't need drawings, because he didn't communicate with anyone.
I found it very strange that they didn't use drawings. You didn't work like that on a shipyard, or on a lathe in a factory. That was a problem for me. They boasted that you couldn't draw it. The things they made were like a violin. In their eyes they were all free forms. Then I started to question their free forms. The kettle was the first product for

As yet I can see only two methods to discover something of the real demand.

The first is that the researcher must be his own counsel as a person, which implies that he himself must use an iron if he is conducting a product analysis of an iron.

The other method is to observe the use of products by others, in which it is not important whether or not the product is complete. Both methods can lead to a more or less clear image of the demand.

The specification

Industrial design is based not only on function but also on the principle that a product can be rationally manufactured.

In order really to be useful for the designer, the guide-lines for the design, which follow from the product analysis, must also be supplemented with those with which the available production apparatus will be set up.

To this specification of guidelines and desires that ensue from both the market and the means of production, we have given the beautiful name 'cahier des charges'.

Wim Gilles, *Industriële vormgeving, de produktanalyse*, 1957

which I used 'form organisation'. Later I wrote a book about that. I predicted then that a time would come when design would consist of fixing measurements in numbers. The most important thing was making forms numerical.

Nowadays everything is driven numerically. The annoying thing is that the real designers (and at the university I worked very hard to change that) don't want to know anything about that. People have no feeling for the theoretical underpinnings of form. In the automotive industry, without exception, things are done in an old-fashioned manner. At the Ford Motor Company they still make a wax model, which is transposed with a laser.

Designing a car is still actually a process of handiwork. What they do, then, is an inverted world. As a designer you are simply an artisan again. It is putting the cart before the horse. To my mind it is like cursing in church.

DRU factory design, coal fire, nineteenth century, cast iron

But does your proposed manner of designing really result in an aesthetically satisfying product? In other words: how non-aesthetic is your kettle, for example?

The kettle has nothing to do with aesthetics. I always compare it to someone who says, "I am a composer and I work as follows: I play something on the piano. I put the tape-recorder on and that is my composition." Bach would turn in his grave if he heard that.

But there is a kind of Gilles style? Or is that cursing in church?

Well, not completely. I think that, in spite of myself, I have still had a style. Maybe I still do. That is your signature, whether it is beautiful or not. What you see is, of course, far from everything. The outward appearance; I do not accept that term as what it is about. It is about presence. I have no control over thoughts about aesthetics. I have always had difficulty with art. Professionalism – that's what I believe in. You can learn that. Industrial design has absolutely nothing to do with art

What is important then?

In my writings I use the term 'generic type'. We recognise things because they have a particular structure. That also has to do with Kant, he also used it. For me this is the essence. If, as a designer, you were asked to design a new version of a particular product then you

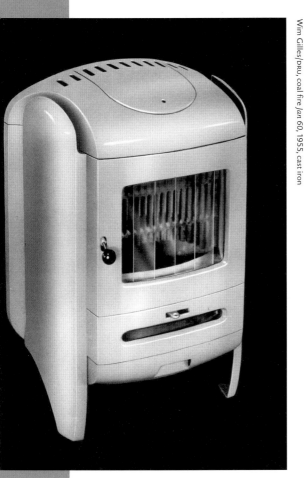

Wim Gilles/DRU, coal fire *Jan 60*, 1955, cast iron

would be well advised to know what the generic type is. If you don't, then you are left holding the baby. A car that doesn't look like a car won't sell.

How 'generic' are your products? And isn't there nonetheless something aesthetic about them?

Well what is an aesthetic rubbish bin? It's a matter of appropriateness, of what is acceptable in the circumstances. There is a bottom line: how ugly may you make something? But I never go further than that.

Is a Rietveld chair also generic?

That depends on the chair.

The Zigzag chair?

No, not that one. That is a type by itself. And it is more symbolic. For me Friso Kramer's 'Revolt' is the ultimate chair. I have never understood why nothing has come of it abroad.

To talk about chairs is automatically to talk of ergonomics.

Am very firm on that point. Chairs are, by definition, not ergonomic. You can never sit well in them, because the chair forces us to adopt a position. You have to keep moving. It is absolutely not comfortable. You have to stay put. We are not made to sit in chairs. You are supposed to squat on your haunches on the ground. A chair is a cultural thing. You have to learn to sit. There is not a single chair that is ergonomically sound.

Anonymous, *rubbish bin*, 1960s, galvanised sheet steel

Friso Kramer/De Cirkel, *Revolt chair*, 1953, sheet steel and plastic, height 78.5 cm

Trellis Wallpaper
1862

Jasmine Wallpaper
1872

Bird Textile
1877-1878

William Morris
(1834-1896)

Morris & Co's works manager related that '… constant watch had to be kept for the effect produced by the necessary repetitions of the pattern on wall or curtain and curious experiences were sometimes had when the repeats of a pattern came to be joined around the original unit. In order to see that all went well therefore it was necessary to have at least parts of eight repeats of the design and sometimes entire repeats carefully drawn round the central 'model'. This precaution made the process of designing very laborious and costly also but Mr Morris never grudged pains or expense in the preparation of his designs.'

George Wardle, *Memorials of William Morris*, p. 189

1
Journal of the Society of Arts, XLVI, May 1898, pp. 629-630

2
Jeffrey maintained dedicated printing logs for the Morris & Co wallpapers. These are now in the Archive of Arthur Sanderson & Sons Ltd.

William Morris was an important figure in Victorian England. He had great energy and enthusiasm, which he brought to bear on his writing, his calligraphy, his printing and his politics. He was also a master of pattern making, with a clear aesthetic vision and a characteristic style. Here, it was his passion for the whole process of making that underpinned his genius. He was able to afford the considerable time and effort involved because he also controlled the company that made (or commissioned) and retailed his designs.

Morris, Marshall, Faulkner & Co was set up in 1861 to offer all aspects of interior decoration. Morris was one of the original founders and in 1875 he became the sole owner and director of the business, which was renamed Morris & Co. The company sold limited editions of specially designed items, but also stock goods made by serial production. Wallpapers were one of the first of the stock ranges.

His earliest wallpaper design, for the *Trellis* pattern, dates from 1862. The trellis motif derives from medieval manuscript illustrations of gardens. The company intended to do its own manufacturing, printing with zinc plates and oil-based inks. However, this was not the usual way of making wallpaper and it proved unworkable. Production was therefore turned over to Jeffrey & Co, an experienced and reputable wallpaper maker.

Jeffrey & Co employed the standard method of hand-block printing with distemper colours. One wooden printing block is cut for each of the colours in the design and each colour is printed consecutively until the pattern is completed. Each block covers the full width of the piece of wallpaper (approx. 52 cm), but has to be applied to the paper again and again to build up the vertical repeat. Great care needs to be taken at all stages – design, block cutting and printing – to make sure the joins do not show.

Morris took an active personal interest in the whole process. Great care needs to be taken in transferring the design to the blocks to make sure that the result remains true to the original and Morris dealt directly with the block cutters rather than leaving it to Jeffrey & Co.[1] Morris would often provide new colourings for existing patterns, but he would not suffer unauthorised changes. However, Jeffrey's printing records also indicate that Morris collaborated on the development of new techniques. There were, for example, numerous failed attempts to print in wash colours before success was achieved.[2]

The design for *Trellis*, though, does not show such attention to detail, either in the drawing of the repeat or the marking of the colours. This is perhaps because it was Morris's earliest attempt and he was still learning about the process. The pattern structure too, is relatively unsophisticated, with little integration of motifs and background and with an obvious repeating unit.

But in the 1870s Morris threw himself anew into wallpaper. The designs themselves became functional working drawings, as can be clearly seen in the *Jasmine* design

William Morris, design for *Jasmine* wallpaper, c. 1872, pencil and watercolour on paper, 90.3 x 64.1 cm

Jasmine wallpaper, woodblock print by Jeffrey & Co for Morris, Marshall, Faulkner & Co, 1872, roll width 68.6 cm

of circa 1872. Here, the paper has been squared-up with guidelines to mark the repeat and the pattern has been extended on three sides to show how it will join.

Morris was well aware that different materials require different types of pattern. Wallpapers, for example, are always seen as flat expanses, but they need to work with other decorative elements in a room. Morris's ideal wall covering presented a surface of subtly broken colour. The *Jasmine* pattern triumphantly achieves this. Morris successfully disguised the repeating unit and created considerable ambiguity between the foreground of jasmine and background of hawthorns.

By the mid-1870s, Morris had effectively conquered the problems of wallpaper design. At this point he turned the full beam of his attention to textiles, printed and then woven. He investigated production methods that would give him the quality he wanted. He rediscovered old dyeing and printing techniques, and eventually took most production into his own hands. He developed a variety of design structures, suited both to the end use of the fabric and to the production processes. The *Bird* textile of 1877-1878, for example, uses a symmetrical 'net' or ogee structure, which neatly repeats horizontally and vertically and is particularly appropriate for weaving. Morris used this fabric to hang the walls of his own drawing room – a decorative finish he personally preferred to wallpaper.

Morris's patterns greatly influenced an entire generation of designers, particularly in Britain and the United States. Moreover, Morris & Co was successfully

William Morris, design for *Bird* textile, 1877-1878, pencil and watercolour on paper, 101.6 x 68.2 cm

Bird textile, 1877-1878, jacquard woven wool for Morris & Co (detail)

innovative in marketing as well as design. Its showroom presented a small but distinctive range of goods – furniture, carpets, papers, textiles and other decorative items – in a coherent and attractive way. It was the first example of a 'lifestyle' shop, showing customers how to assemble the 'look'. The serially produced wallpapers and textiles were not outrageously costly and they successfully appealed to the comfortably-off intellectual or artistic middle classes, perhaps most acutely stereotyped by the academic households of Oxford.

Literature

Linda Parry (ed.), *William Morris*, London 1996

Paperclip

Anonymous
Second half
of the
nineteenth
century

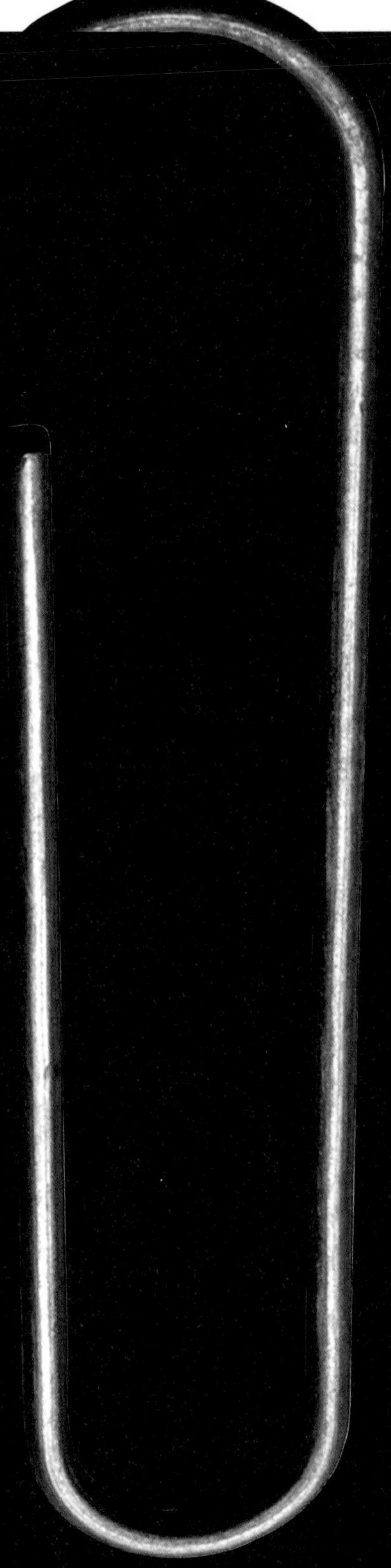

1899

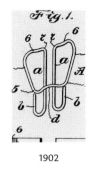

1902

1903

1903

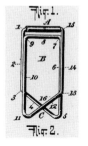

1904

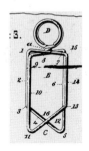

1904

1904

1904

1904

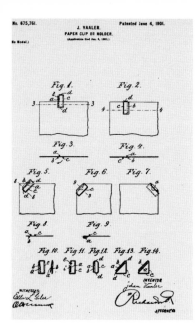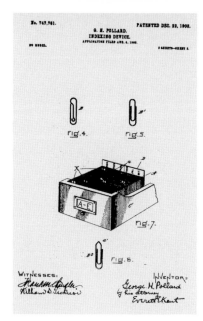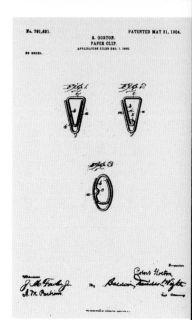

Three patents for paperclips from 1901, 1903 and 1904 respectively

Design critics often cite the paperclip as an exemplar of simplicity and suitability – a perfect example of the modernist maxim: 'form follows function'. This actually appears to be more ambiguous. Patent applications for paperclips provide such a rich diversity of forms – all of them more or less satisfactory – that the paperclip actually undermines this claim.

H. Petroski, 'The Evolution of Artifacts', *American Scientist*, vol. 80, Sept./Oct. 1992, p. 420

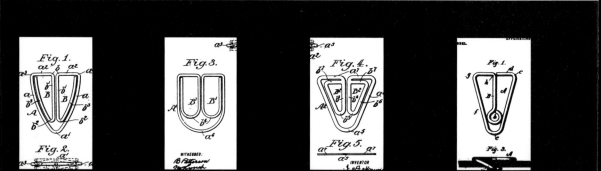

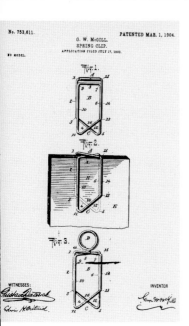
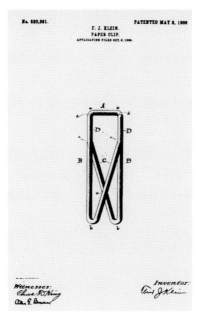
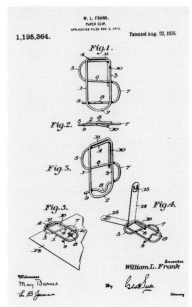

Three patents for paperclips from 1904, 1906 and 1916 respectively

The paperclip was made possible only by the availability of steel wire. It is based on 'Hooke's Law' of physics published by the English scientist Robert Hooke in 1679: *Ut tensio, sic uis* (as is the extension, so is the force). Or in other words: a force exerted on a spring, returns with equal force. A paperclip always wants to return to its original position and it is this elasticity that makes it so suitable for its purpose.

H. Petroski, *The Evolution of Useful Things*, New York 1993, p. 59

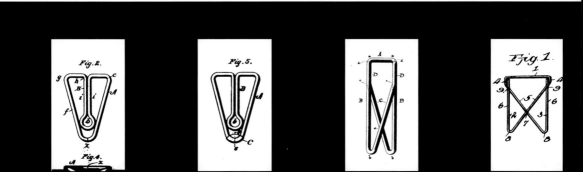

Each year manufactures produce some twenty thousand million paperclips.[1] In addition to bundling papers together, they also serve as tie-pins, as stocking fasteners, for cleaning fingernails and ears, or for playing with during meetings. Just like the crown cap, the clothes peg, the roll-shutter, the blister pack and the roofing tile – the list is endless – they are wonders of technology and ingenuity. They appear trustworthy and anonymous, as if they had always existed. But appearances are not everything. They were also designed, and often not so very long ago.

The paperclip dates from the second half of the nineteenth century. At that time people affixed papers with a pin, which had a number of drawbacks: it held together merely a few sheets and it damaged the papers; it was also time consuming and required considerable dexterity. People often pricked their fingers, especially when thumbing quickly through a pile of papers. Around 1850 – when bureaucratisation was growing apace – sheet-metal paperclips came onto the market. They were relatively cumbersome constructions, not dissimilar to the bulldog or alligator clips used on clipboards today. Some of them bit into the paper, thus damaging it. It was not until the invention of malleable steel wire that it was possible to produce the paperclip as we know it today. They existed in many variations and benefited from the fact that they were easy to attach and held many sheets together, which, moreover, they no longer damaged.

It is not known precisely when the paperclip was introduced. Encyclopædias give the Norwegian Johan Vaaler as the inventor, but the American engineer Henry Petroski discovered during his thorough study of patents that the matter is more complicated.[2]

Vaaler patented his invention in 1899. His paperclip superficially resembles the model that we use today, however, there is another clip that bears closer similarities to the current paperclip. It is the so-called 'Gem', which is anonymous and undated, but certainly older than Vaaler's patent. Petroski unearthed it by chance. In a patent application for a machine for making paperclips, dated 27 April 1899, it is casually illustrated, without a name or an attribution, from which Petroski concludes that it

1
This figure is based on data from 1993. See: H. Petroski, *The Evolution of Useful Things*, 1993, p. 52

2
Henry Petroski is an engineer and regular columnist for American Scientist. He specialises in the study of everyday products and continually poses surprising and stimulating questions about the origins of these things. The information in this article has been assembled from the many articles he wrote on the subject

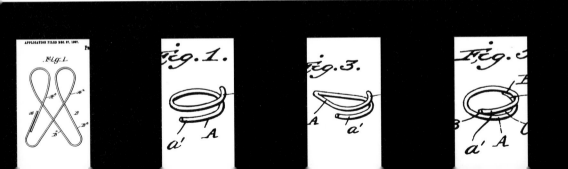

during the
1990s. See:
H. Petroski,
The Evolution
of Artifacts',
American
Scientist,
vol. 80,
Sept/Oct 1992,
pp. 416-421

3
H. Petroski,
On Dating
Inventions',
American
Scientist,
vol. 81,
July/Aug 1993,
pp. 314-317

was already in general use. Unlike Vaaler's clip, which had merely a single loop, the Gem consisted of a double loop. The Gem, probably named after the British manufacturer Gem Limited, became the standard for the paperclip.

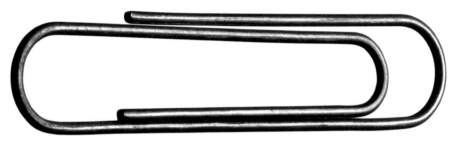

In Norway during the Second World War paperclips, so the story goes, were a symbol of resistance. The Norwegians wore them on their lapels to show their patriotism: the accredited inventor of the paperclip was Norwegian. It also symbolised the power of solidarity and resilience.
H. Petroski, *The Evolution of Useful Things*, New York 1993, p. 60

Everyday implements are often the result of a lengthy evolutionary process, as people attempt time and again to improve existing objects.[3] Vaaler's clip benefited from the fact that it did not become entangled with other clips in its packaging, but was awkward to attach. The Gem slid easily onto the paper but stuck together in the box, whilst the sharp ends damaged the paper. As early as 1900 the American Cornelius Brosnan applied for a patent for his 'Konaclip'. He formed the inner wire into an eyelet, so that the clip no longer pricked the paper and was easy to attach. However, sheets easily came loose, particularly from the middle of the pile. In 1902 Alfred Shedlock of Jersey City patented the 'Ideal' clip, especially suited to thick bundles of paper. Three years later Joshua Hale from Providence applied for a patent for the 'Ring' clip, a round paperclip consisting of two circles, which has remained

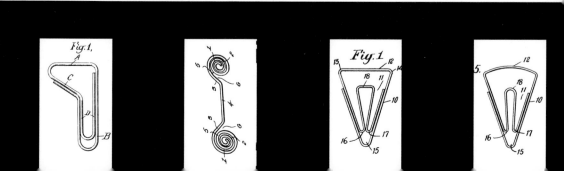

Gem, the standard for the paperclip, design before 1899, steel wire

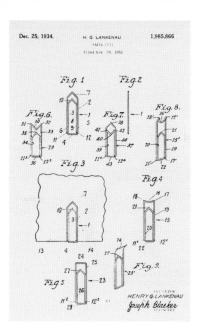

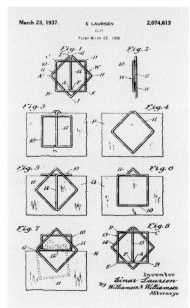

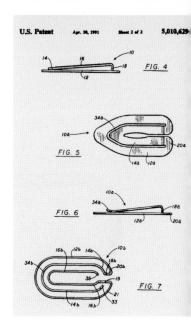

Three patents for paperclips from 1934, 1937 and 1991 respectively

in constant use. In 1934 Henry Lankenau was granted a patent for a paperclip that, in certain details, was an improvement upon the Gem. He flattened off one side and formed the other into a V-shape. He called it the 'Gothic' as a reaction to the Roman-looking Gem. Despite the Gothic's better performance, the Gem has become the standard.

Although the Gothic left little room for improvement, it was not the end of the story. People continue to apply for patents for new discoveries. In the 1950s plastic clips appeared, in many colours, but with limited elasticity. There are also steel wire clips covered with a layer of coloured plastic. They are less handy that the ordinary metal clips, but nonetheless they continue to sell. Dissatisfied with the Gem, which clips onto the paper from only one side, Charles Link designed the 'Endless Filament' in 1991. Like this clip, the history of the development of the paperclip appears also to be endless.

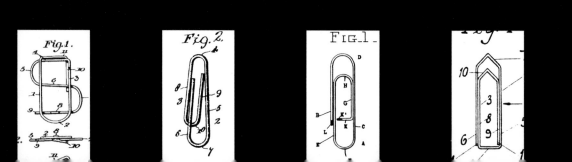

The predecessor of the paperclip, the peg,
has a long history and dates back to 3000 BC.
The Sumerians used metal pins to fasten their
clothes. They were made by hand, a time-
consuming process that moreover led to
irksome variations in quality. Around 1835
the American John Ireland Howe managed to
produce them mechanically: 'bank-pins' for
banknotes and 'toilette' pins for clothing.
The former he supplied loose, per half pound,
the latter pinned to cards so that you could
immediately see that the tips were good and
that you had been given the correct amount.
The bank-pins sometimes had a T-shaped
head so that they were easier to fish out of
the pile and so that they did not slip through
the paper.

H. Petroski, *The Evolution of Useful Things*, New York 1993, pp. 54-57

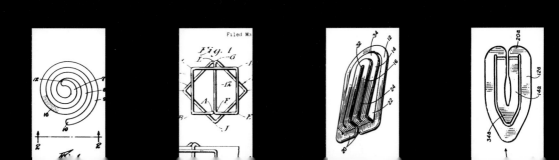

Odol Bottle 1893

Karl Lingner (1861-1916)
ascribed to

Odol advertising bottle, screenprinted glass, 1920s, height 12.2 cm

In 1891 the autodidact and self-made man Karl August Lingner (1861-1916) befriended the chemist Dr. Richard Seifert, who opened up for him the world of modern bacteriology, introduced him to his scientific colleagues and gave him the recipe for an antibiotic remedy, the closely-guarded secret ingredients of which would become Odol mouthwash.

In October 1892 Lingner established his own company, the Dresdner Chemische Laboratorium, and began production of Odol. He used a unique advertising and promotion strategy, based on an American model, ranging from painted advertisements on Zeppelins and building facades to advertisements in the daily press. Due to the unusually original design and the remarkably truthful advertisements for that time, the product turned out to be a succes from the very beginning. In the history of modern marketing he has earned his place as the 'father of branding'.

Odol smells of

Odol and of Germany

In the world of packaging, where according to the marketing books packaging should change every five years, twenty-five years is an exception. A 110-year-old bottle design is a huge exception. One such bottle is the most surreal, wilful and impossible sort every designed: inconspicuous and still known to everyone: the bottle for Odol mouthwash (1893).

Odol has its origins in the social and scientific developments of the end of the nineteenth century. It was the time in which Robert Koch identified the tuberculosis bacillus and the results of Louis Pasteur's research were made public. In the production of foodstuffs hygiene was still a rare commodity. The general public had little knowledge of the bacterial cause of diseases. Large parts of the working classes lived in wretched conditions and were housed in accommodation of which General Booth, the founder of the Salvation Army, once said that you would not even keep a London cab horse. Unchecked by any laws, at the end of the nineteenth century a number of medicines were launched on the market that often contained little more than a high percentage of alcohol and opium. Standards of oral hygiene were also bad. Ninety per cent of children between the ages of six and fourteen had lost twenty per cent of their teeth. No wonder that Odol mouthwash, with its believable, simple message and antibiotic effects was such a rapid success, even though a single bottle cost almost as much as most working-class families could afford to spend on soap and other sanitary products in a month.

That success was not restricted to Germany – Odol was soon being produced in twenty countries and was available in sixty. This popularity would probably not have been possible without the idiosyncratic bottle that remained unchanged from 1893 until 1954. The use of milk-white or opal glass made it extra special. The original sealed patent stopper was in due course replaced by a modern screw top. The bottle is, all in all, a classic of international design and is in many ways comparable with the Coca-Cola bottle. We know the name of the Coca-Cola bottle's designer but the author of the Odol bottle is unknown. In all probability it was the inventor Karl Lingner himself. The bottle was patented only in 1907. In this sense it also bears comparison with the Coca-Cola bottle, which was introduced in 1916 but which was registered as a trademark only in 1960. But this is where the comparison ends. Where Coca-Cola stood for youth and American freedom, Odol stood for reliability and German cleanliness.

Odol smells of Odol and of Germany. In this sense the product was popular in Germany not only before the Second World War, but it also fitted the *Gesundes Volk* campaign during the Nazi period. After 1945 the product was once again warmly embraced as a symbol of pre-war Germany.

The early success very quickly spurned copies. An Odol advertisement of 1907 shows thirty-three imitations with names such as Dentol, Odentol and Odalline, six of which employed a similar type of bottle to that used by Odol. It was undoubtedly

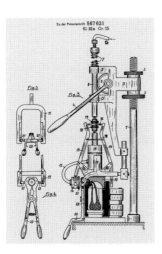

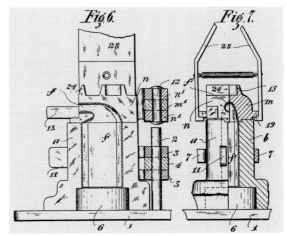

Illustration of the production of the *Odol* bottle from patent 567 621, 1931

a challenge for the glass industry to work out how such a bottle could be made. Apparently the practical problem solving methods of a bicycle manufacturer had to be employed. At the European Patents Office in The Hague a number of patents were filed to make bottles with the neck bent to one side. These were invariably for one and the same bottle: the Odol mouthwash bottle or something that was supposed to pass for it. In 1919 the Alexandra Bottle Works in Glasgow, where bottles were still made with a blowpipe, patented a hinge with a lid that could be drawn over the bottle's relatively weak upper section. In 1931 Hermann Meier from Markt-leuthen, Oberfranken, applied for a patent to make Odol bottles using his own method on a semi-automatic machine. The beautiful drawings for the 'Patentschrift 567621' still inspire delight amongst enthusiasts. They show how, after the pre-moulding phase, still hanging in the pincers that form the bottle's mouth, they reached their final form. After that a lever was lowered whereby, in a single motion, the neck of the bottle was bent and the blowhead was pressed against the mouth, through which the compressed air created the form.

As early as 1919 the most successful manufacturer of semi-automatic bottle machines, Adolf Schiller of Berlin- Schöneberg, patented a method of introducing the compressed air directly into the side of the mould. That was a revolutionary approach to the manufacture of what one can safely call an perverse model of bottle. Just as anyone who wants to open a bottle, bottle makers are also inclined to begin at the top.

Odol bottles are still made in Momignies in Belgium and by the Italian firm Bormioli in Parma. How they are made remains a trade secret. The cocky little centenarian continues to baffle the technicians.

literature

E. Leitherer, H. Wichmann, *Gestaltete Warenverpackungen des 19. und 20. Jahrhunderts*, Stuttgart 1987

M. Scheske, M. Roth, H.-C. Taubrich, *In Aller Munde. Einhundert Jahre Odol*, Dresden 1993

J. Soetens, *Verpakt in Glas/Packaged in Glass*, Amsterdam 2001

Dinner and Serving Cutlery circa 1895-1900

P.J.H. Cuypers (1827-1921)

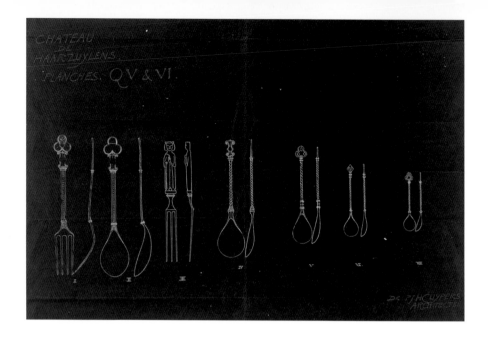

The building that Pierre Cuypers reconstructed on the foundations of the mediaeval ruin of Castle De Haar in Haarzuilen, including all outbuildings and the extensive grounds, is one of the few *Gesamtkunstwerken* in the Netherlands. The complex, which is a romanticised nineteenth-century vision of the Middle Ages, is of exceptional importance. Cuypers took charge not only of the architecture, which he extended, brought up to date and modernised, but also the interiors and all furnishings and fittings. In the second half of the nineteenth century Cuypers had attained considerable fame for his plans for the Rijksmuseum (1876) and the Central Station (1881), both in Amsterdam. Because of his eclectic historicist style he was the obvious choice to restore De Haar to its former glory.

As early as 1887 there had already been plans to rebuild the castle. The ruin was bequeathed to Etienne, Baron van Zuylen van Nijevelt (1860-1934) in 1890 and in that same year he, together with his wife Hélène, Baroness de Rothschild (1864-1947), commissioned Cuypers to draw up new plans for the castle and everything associated with it. His first design dates from 1891 and in total he would work on its realisation for almost forty years.

The cutlery service is extremely extensive. In addition to the usual items of flatware including fish knives and dessert cutlery in great numbers, it also included cutlery for cheese, ginger etc. The serving implements are also richly varied, including tart servers, sugar tongs, butter knives, custard ladles and croquette servers. The sixty or so components provide an insight into the nineteenth-century design and production processes. Cuypers designed a great many variants, in which heraldry played a visually determining role. Just as with everything else in the castle, he also applied the Van Zuylen family's crest to the cutlery. On an unrealised design he even added

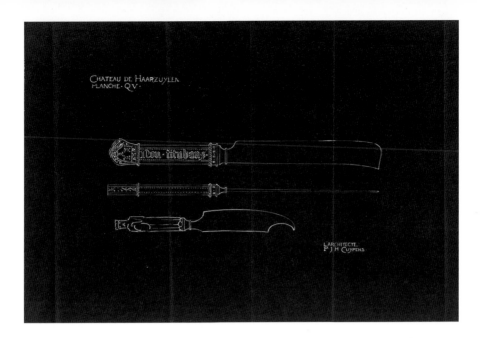

their motto 'Non Titubans'. Each item of cutlery – with the exception of those pieces with a mother-of-pearl handle – bear the arms of the Van Zuylens.

Every piece of cutlery has a heart-shaped tail that sprouts a motif of three leaves. This tail is ajour, and shows the family's standard between expressive tracery. Many of the handles are smooth and are sometimes interrupted by a leaf motif. The connections between the stem and the bowl of the spoon and the tines of the fork are often reinforced with a classical rat's tail. Some items, such as the fish knives and forks, and many of the serving pieces have a decorative perforated pattern. The cutlery is even more richly varied by the partial gilding of some elements of the individual pieces.

The cutlery was made by the renowned Parisian workshops of Cardeilhac. Apparently there were no silversmiths in the Netherlands that could produce work of a similar quality. Cuypers would not have elaborated each and every piece in detail, but would have left much to the discretion of the silversmiths, relying upon their extensive experience and knowledge. Unrealisable details would not even have been altered through consultation. Various pieces, such as the sugar tongs, appear simply to have been part of Cardeilhac's standard collection. Only in the application of the coat-of-arms do they become a part of the whole.

literature

Exh.cat., 'De lelijke tijd', pronkstukken van Nederlandse interieurkunst 1835-1895, Amsterdam (Rijksmuseum) 1996, pp. 262-264

Kombinationsteekanne 1923

Theodor Bogler (1897-1968)

Theodor Bogler, *Kombinationssteekkanne* with cross-braced handle and eccentric lid, cast and assembled stoneware, nickel silver, rattan, 1923, height 12.5 cm

The Bauhaus founded in Weimar by Walter Gropius in 1919 was destined to become arguably the twentieth century's most influential school of design, thanks to the input of such teaching staff as Lyonel Feininger, Johannes Itten, Wassily Kandinsky, Paul Klee, Gerhard Marcks, Laszlo Moholy-Nagy and Oskar Schlemmer. Its outstanding achievements in the fields of art education, fine art, design, stage and architecture made it the leading professional design school in the world. The teaching concept of this avant-garde institution was informed by a pluralistic approach that involved experimentation, training in creativity, and teamwork in a hands-on workshop environment. With his call for a new unity of art and technology, Gropius gave the Bauhaus a future-oriented framework in 1922, turning the Bauhaus workshops into 'laboratories for industry', where students developed models and prototypes, some of them worth patenting, that are still regarded as early design classics – among them the Jucker and Wagenfeld table lamps, Marcel Breuer's furniture for children, and textiles by Gunta Stölzl. Instead of emulating academic tradition and the accepted canon of style, the Bauhaus fostered inventiveness and innovation in materials, technology, function and form as an expression of modern industrial society. Attracting a cosmopolitan array of teachers and up to twenty-five per cent foreign students, the Bauhaus became a meeting place for the European avant-garde, and maintained close contacts with the Dutch *De Stijl* movement, as represented, most notably, by Theo van Doesburg's course at Weimar in 1922.

The ceramics workshop at the Bauhaus was headed by the sculptor Gerhard Marcks and from 1920 was housed in the long-established pottery workshop of Max Krehan at Dornburg an der Saale, some thirty kilometres from Weimar. Apart from the traditional training provided in Krehan's workshop, a second workshop dedicated to developing new and innovative approaches to ceramics design was established in the former royal stables of the Dornburg Palace complex, which also served as a student residence. Some important graduates of the Bauhaus ceramics workshop were Werner Burri, Johannes Driesch, Johannes Lessmann, Wilhelm Löber, Marguerite Friedlaender, Margarete Heymann-Marks and Franz Rudolf Wildenhain. In the spring of 1923 the most talented students and recently qualified potters, Theodor Bogler and Otto Lindig, contacted ceramics and porcelain companies and began gathering experience in ceramics casting techniques. In doing so, they deliberately made the leap from the craft techniques of the potter's wheel to the field of industrial technology, and set up a workshop where plaster models could be produced.

In the spring of 1923, Theodor Bogler developed the first design family in the Bauhaus ceramics workshop: household ceramics, flasks, storage jars, pots and even coffeemakers, as well as his famous modular teapots. It is no coincidence that the standard model designations (L1-L6) for the ceramics workshop were introduced with these serially produced items, given that they so ideally embodied the creative principles and concepts of modern design. Apart from his quest for functional

variety, Bogler also addressed the problem of the uniformity of mass-produced products and developed strategic solutions to tackle this particular problem. In order to achieve a wide diversity of formal variations, he took as his starting point the functional elements of the pot: handle, opening and spout. Apart from the traditional handle form, he also introduced a tubular handle on the side of the pot, and perforated ceramic elements designed to hold a variety of metal or nickerwork handles. The opening of the pot could be either centred or off-centre, in combination with a funnel element and several strained insets. Moreover, the actual body of the pot itself consisted of a cylinder and an upward or downward facing hemisphere, whereby the diameter of the base ring was always the same as that of the opening. Finally, he created three different spout positions – at the top, middle and bottom of the cylinder. Of all the theoretically possible variations in form, more than ten were actually chosen and applied to the large teapot and produced as limited-run prototypes, having been 'tested' beforehand as to function and form. By applying different glazes and glazing techniques, these otherwise identical industrially produced teapots became unique one-offs. Given the aptness of Theodor Bogler's first 'design family' as a response to the issues of modern industrial design,

the lukewarm response with which these products were met at the Leipzig and Frankfurt trade fairs must have seemed all the more galling. Sales did not meet expectations. Walter Gropius' visionary aim of supplying the broad mass of the public with beautiful, functional, affordable and durable products, created using a minimum of material and energy, seemed to have failed because their form was too experimental. This perceived feedback was immediately channelled into new product ideas by Bogler and Lindig. The tea set (L 40-42) and a series of coffeepots by Lindig (L 10-L 16) were given more overtly organic forms, closer to those of historical models. Horizontal grooves were even added to the body of the pot, echoing the traditional craftsmanship of the potter's wheel. This development culminated in Otto Lindig's coffee pot (L 19), produced in 1923 in both stoneware and porcelain and manufactured by Aelteste Volkstedter Porzellanfabrik. They demonstrated an exemplary combination of innovation and tradition, heralding a phase of 'new

simplicity' at the Bauhaus, which was also evident in the products of the other Bauhaus workshops. The Bauhaus Style of 1923 was superseded by more open design concepts.

literature
Klaus Weber (ed.), *Keramik und Bauhaus*, Berlin 1989
Michael Siebenbrodt (ed.), *Bauhaus Weimar, Entwürfe für die Zukunft*, Ostfildern Ruit 2000

Archival photograph from the album *Bauhaus Pottery*, Volume IV / Supplement / page 23, 4 tea pots, Theodor Bogler, c.1923

Ram Ceramics 1919-1926

Th.A.C. Colenbrander (1841-1930)

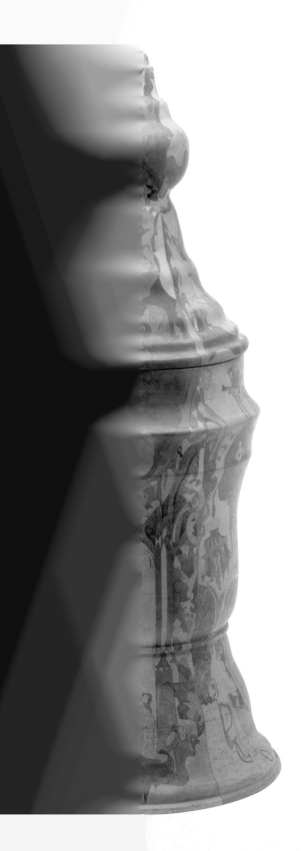

Aim and endeavour: humanity united with its environment. Peace on earth must be achieved. I believe that true material beauty shall continue to support this aim, but vain pomp and splendour is depraved. Away with rubbish and fripperies

Colenbrander, 28 February 1919

T.A.C. Colenbrander/Ram, biscuit model for lidded vase with 1/8 part *Cathedral* decoration, c.1925, earthenware with watercolour, height 59 cm

It is almost inconceivable that the unbridled production of more than sixty ceramic items and seven hundred different decorations, produced within seven years for the Plateelbakkerij De Ram in Arnhem, may be attributed to a man who was nearing his eightieth year. Nonetheless, at this advanced age Colenbrander succeeded in assembling just such an extensive collection and in so doing gave new impulse to the production of decorated industrial ceramics in the Netherlands.

Colenbrander, trained as an architect, attained international recognition towards the end of the nineteenth century with his highly personal ceramics, which he developed for Rozenburg between 1884 and 1889. In the following years he devoted himself mainly to carpet designs for various weavers. Around 1914 he worked on new models for the Plateelbakkerij Zuid-Holland. Both his two and three-dimensional work exhibits an extremely strong individuality and originality. He managed to fuse motifs, mainly from nature, and in a single case from architecture, into a shimmering whole of wellnigh hallucinatory abstract motifs, often executed in surprising marriages of colour.

The manner in which he makes drawings of flowers – reducing the flowers to their primitive forms; unpicking them, lengthening, widening them; all dependent on the demands of the forms of the vases and dishes; always consistent with the form; retaining the weak limpness of picked petals; deeply contemporary in concept; never stiff, as in the lotus flower or later the fleur-de-lys, which are used rather as an infinitely repeated decoration – is admirable.

Anonymous contemporary review

In his designs he deployed the repetition, rotation and mirroring of patterns – conventional methods for applying surface ornament at the time. Colenbrander repeated asymmetrical patterns four, six or twelve times on beakers and vases. In a single case he mirrored a pattern three times, thereby creating a symmetrical decoration. There are also vases entirely enveloped with a single asymmetrical motif and plates and bowls the entire surface of which is filled with an asymmetrical pattern or a motif repeated three, four of five times.

In 1919 he began the difficult task of developing new ceramic forms and decorations under the best possible conditions imaginable from a technical standpoint: in

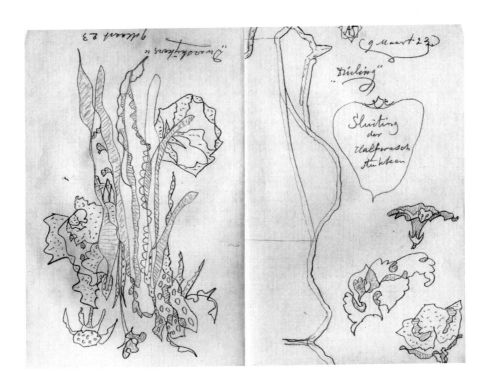

T.A.C. Colenbrander, *Peeping Tom* and *Triplet* decorations, 9 March 1923, pencil on paper, 20 x 28 cm

his own factory, financed by devoted friends and supported by the best craftsmen. He invested an unprecedented amount of time in the development of new glazes.

Colenbrander's working method was as follows. Firstly he drew the profiles of models on paper, which were used to form a matrix from a turned block of plaster. This served as the basis for a removable, multipartite plaster mould in which clay could be cast. Once dried, these cast models would be fired. This is known as a biscuit model, which can thereafter be glazed.

Colenbrander designed his patterns firstly on paper and then on a biscuit model. He drew the decorations with pencil and filled them in with paint. Because the patterns repeated themselves on a particular form, a number of decorations could be applied very efficiently in segments to a single model. These working models served as the

T.A.C. Colenbrander, biscuit model for dish with *Floating* decoration, 1922-1925, earthenware with watercolour, Ø 41.5 cm (detail)

T.A.C. Colenbrander, biscuit model for a bowl with *Iris blossom, Brilliant and Notting* decorations, c.1925, earthenware with watercolour, Ø 18.5 cm

And then so many visions and individual flower drawings flew from me, that it was a great struggle to get through them.

Letter from Colenbrander to Hulsbergen, 11 June 1919

proofs for the decorator, who transferred the pattern through a unique, patented process onto the models to be glazed. For transferring the patterns he did not employ the usual perforated paper stencils, through which charcoal stipples are applied to the ceramics. Instead De Ram developed a supple, translucent, cellulose film, which was an impression of the biscuit model. First the decorator applied the contours in black and then filled them in with enamel glazes like a colour plate. These opaque glazes could be applied directly adjacent to each other and there were no visible brush marks. The glazed model could then be fired for a second time in the kiln. The only disadvantage was that the glaze was difficult to apply to the biscuit model.

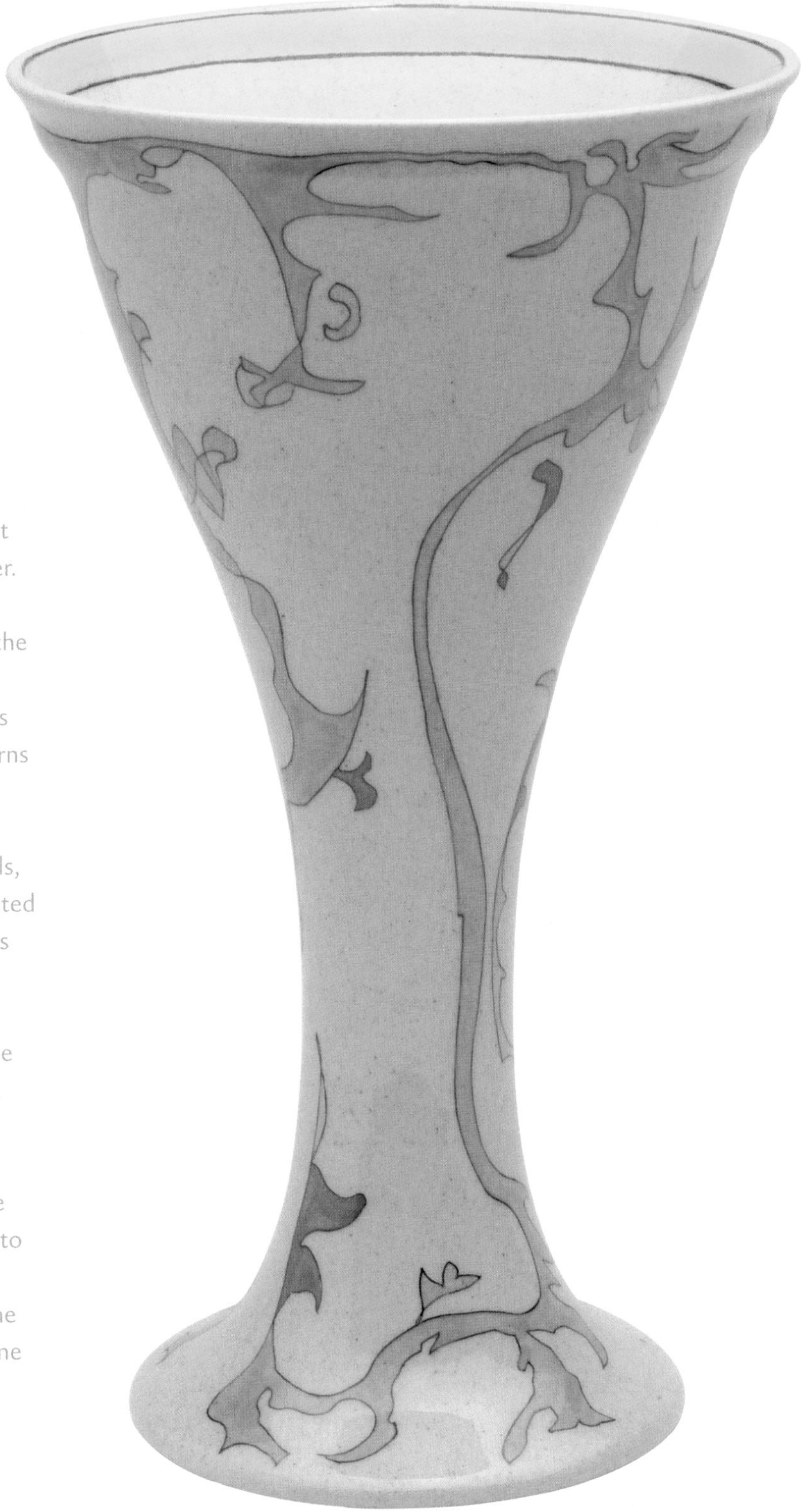

T.A.C. Colenbrander/Ram, *Spindly vase*, 1925, earthenware, height 22.2 cm

…Yesterday in the drawing shop […] I met with Willem, the painter. […] It will be another good fortnight before the firing can take place, because Willem still has to transfer all my patterns (which are now on the model vases) onto an equal number of models, which when I have painted again with watercolours and varnished, will henceforth serve as models for copies of the pieces to go in the kiln. It is much work, but progress is swift. My original patterns on the model vases then go into the archive and can be copied again, in case the copy models suffer some wear and tear…

Letter from Colenbrander to Hulsbergen, 31 March 1921

Colenbrander was very satisfied with the quality that he achieved at De Ram, where his quest for the optimum combination of clay, glazes and firing process reached a highpoint. In his last known letter, written shortly before his death, he concluded, not without a little pathos:

Everything is achieved.

Letter from Colenbrander to Hulsbergen, 30 July 1929

T.A.C. Colenbrander/Ram, *Cathedral garniture*, 1925, earthenware, height 57 cm

At De Ram they also worked with oxide paints, entirely against Colenbrander's wishes:

The oxyde paints […] can be applied more thinly than mine, but they are always uneven – like watercolours. That is something that my patterns cannot suffer; 'tis shoddy work.

Letter from Colenbrander to Hulsbergen, undated, after 1924

64

Museum Boijmans Van Beuningen owns the archive
of D.J. Hulsbergen (1894-1965), which provides great
insight into Colenbrander's activities. It includes two
cases from 1922 with glazed tiles. These served as
colour samples for the composition of each
decoration's palette. From the total of seventy-three
colours Colenbrander eventually selected thirty-six.
There are also two small boxes with fired biscuit proofs.
In addition there is a large group of model drawings
and designs for decorations and an extensive
correspondence between Hulsbergen and
Colenbrander concerning various thorny issues such as
the financing of the new factory, the development of
new models, the composition of the clay, the workshop,
the assistants, the fired biscuit proofs etc.

01 Olive green
02 Straw yellow
03 Blush
04 White
05 Blazing red
06 Dark blue
07 Golden yellow
08 Violet
09 Mauve
10 Lilac
11 Spring green
12 Winter green
13 Copper
14 Brass
15 Verdigris
16 Chestnut yellow
17 Lead blue
18 Aquamarine
19 Turquoise
20 Rose
21 Orange
22 Berry juice
23 Dark blue
24 Blue
25 Yellow
26 Winter
27 Vermilion
28 Cornflower blue
29 Turquoise
30 Dark purple
31 Dark red
32 Lilac (frost)
33 Summer green
34 Blazing red
35 Gold

36 Bronze
37 Flesh colour
38 Mauve
39 Spring green
40 Pale green
41 Aurora
42 Sand
43 Flesh colour (pinkish red)
44 Cornflower blue
45 Pale green
46 Winter green
47 Grey
48 Bronze
49 Dark green
50 Blue
51 Black
52 Blood red
53 Turquoise
54 Matt gold
55 Red
56 Bright green
57 Green
58 Red
59 Red
60 Dark red
61 Red
62 Moss green
63 Moss green (dark)
64 Red (light)
65 Green (blue)
66 Vermilion
67 Red
68 Turquoise (dark)
69 Napels yellow
70 Pale yellow
71 Blue (Turquoise)
72 Bronze
73 Light Bronze

Ram, case with glaze proofs, 1922

Ram, case with glaze proofs, 1922

Ram, biscuit proofs, 1923

I sit now full of surprise and admiration with the boxes next to me that contain a small new world, into which life must be blown. The essence is already there, it lacks only the correct means of expression.

Colenbrander, 29 July 1923

literature

Exh.cat., *T.A.C. Colenbrander (1841-1930), Plateelbakkerij 'RAM' te Arnhem*, Arnhem (Gemeentemuseum) 1987

R. Mills, 'Motif and Variations: A study of Dutch Art Nouveau Ceramic and Carpet Designs by T.A.C. Colenbrander', *Studies in the Decorative Arts*, IV (1996-1997) I, pp. 85-117

T.M. Eliens, *T.A.C. Colenbrander (1841-1930) ontwerper van de Haagse Plateelbakkerij Rozenburg*, Zwolle 1999

Jaarbeker
1924-1925

H.P. Berlage
(1856-1934)

… May I also enquire of you whether you have already been able to find time for the Anniversary goblet or other commemorative object, of which I previously enquired? …

Letter from Berlage to Cochius, 18 September 1924

… Concerning the anniversary goblet, I can inform you that I have prepared a provisional sketch, with which I shall provide you upon my return…

Letter from Berlage to Cochius, 18 September 1924

The Glasfabriek Leerdam, founded in 1878, has played a leading role in the history of Dutch design. It was not only one of the first factories to work with artists on a large scale, it also actively promoted closer working relationships between other industries and artists in order to ensure better products. This idealistic pursuit formed the basis for the establishment of associations of designers and manufacturers such as the Union for Art and Industry (BKI), founded in 1924. A driving force behind this reform was the Glasfabriek's enlightened director P.M. Cochius (1878-1938), who combined the theosophical heritage with socialist utopianism.

The products of this artistic collaboration form an important part of Museum Boijmans Van Beuningen's collection of applied arts. Initially they included mainly drinks and breakfast services and vases. Latterly they include the anniversary goblets that the Glasfabriek Leerdam issued between 1918 and 1928, which belonged to the company's range of prestige objects. The first four were designed by K.P.C. de Bazel (1869-1923). The last of these, designed in 1922 and issued posthumously in 1924, was the most elaborate. It is a lavishly crafted goblet-vase in purple crystal with a gilded legend on the rim. The first three (1918, 1919 and 1920) were much simpler. In 1924, when Berlage was asked to continue this tradition, the production of the goblets was raised to a higher technical and artistic level.

Possibly mindful of submitting it to the *Exposition Des Arts Décoratifs Modernes* in Paris in 1925, Berlage designed a tall goblet vase with unrivalled presence and style for the Netherlands at that time.[1] In 1926 he designed a heptagonal goblet-vase in purple crystal, its rim consisting of seventy cut facets, signifying Berlage's age at the time.

In 1928 A.D. Copier (1901-1991), the factory's resident designer, produced a pentagonal goblet commemorating the Glasfabriek's fiftieth anniversary, in which he incorporated the firm's logo – three triangles forming a larger triangle – as a decorative element.

The design process of the anniversary goblet can be followed in four drawings. The earliest of these bears the title 'SKETCH DESIGN FOR AN ANNIVERSARY GOBLET 1825' (sic). It is the largest drawing of the series, and was probably intended for presentation because, unlike the others, it is elaborated with charcoal and coloured pencils. The design, a lidded goblet with great presence, already exhibits many of the definitive model's features. A noticeable difference is that this design is pentagonal, whilst the final version is octagonal. Moreover, the proportions are on the whole somewhat more squat. The design also has a richly decorated exterior, some details of which were unrealisable – the diamond-cutting on the corners of the belly and a complicated star-shaped pinnacle could not be produced. The knob is based on a dodecahedron, a regular polyhedron of twelve pentagons.

1
The Glasfabriek Leerdam made an extensive submission to the Paris Exposition in 1925. Unfortunately it is not known whether the goblet was included.

This drawing shows Berlage's proportional strategy very precisely. He employed a system of concentric circles, into which he fitted regular pentagons and decagons. Berlage used the circles not only to define the diameter of the foot, belly and the lid, but he also set a number of them above each other to determine the height of the various parts. This gave the vase harmonic spatial proportions which, in his eyes, contributed to the beauty of the design. Like many of the other designers in Leerdam, Berlage employed this sort of proportional strategy to achieve a rational, universal beauty. Such systems refer to universal relationships, of which the golden section is the best known.

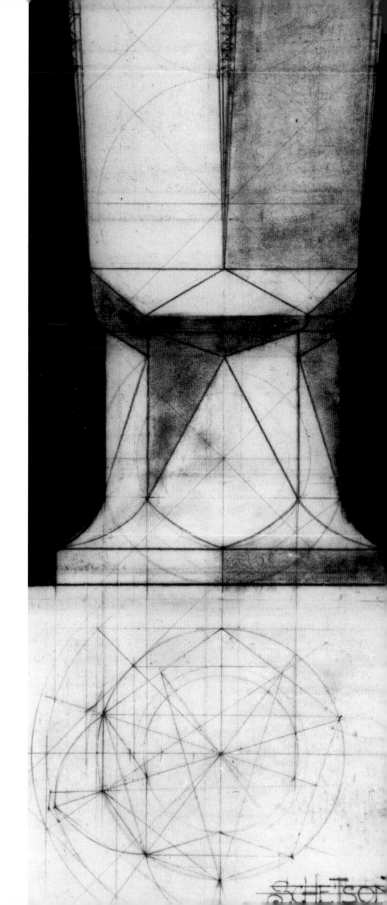

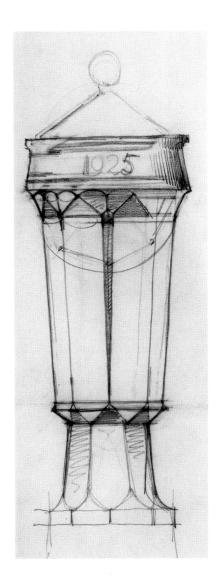

A subsequent sketch displays greater similarities with the final, sober design. The octagon is introduced as the basis, the proportions are modified and the diamond-cutting is replaced with a sandblasted band. There are other alterations such as a spherical knob crowning the lid, and the foot now consists of eight cut sections instead of triangular facets. The transition between the foot and the belly also shows a technically complicated sharp edge.

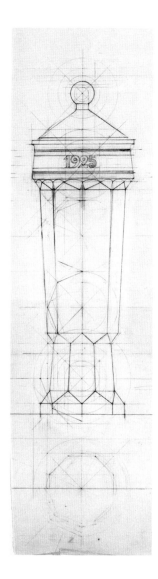

It is clear that the quick sketch served as the basis for this more finished drawing. The unrealisable edge and the curved planes of the foot have disappeared. Through these simplifications the design makes a more slender impression.

The final design, which comes closest to the definitive object, shows that Berlage has made the form more elegant. The octagon remains. The foot now consists of alternating curved triangles, whilst the transition to the body of the goblet has acquired a simpler solution. Berlage has reduced his employment of cut triangles. It is noteworthy that the lid has acquired an octagonal knob echoing the principal form.

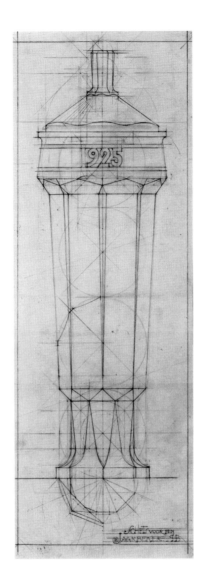

In this drawing Berlage's proportional strategy is once again clearly visible. Within the elevation he incorporated five circles, the uppermost of which shares its heart with that of the spherical knob. One can also see that the various circles mark other crucial points, such as the cut of the foot and the position of the legend.

Because the final design still differs from the definitive version, one may assume that a definitive drawing must have existed. This drawing, bearing the legend 'To The New Age 1925' in angular capitals, appears to have been lost.

literature
Thimo te Duits, 'De jaarbekers van de Glasfabriek Leerdam (1918-1928)', *Antiek*, vol. 27 (1992) no. 1, pp. 17-31

Vases 1928-1929

Frank Lloyd Wright (1868-1959)

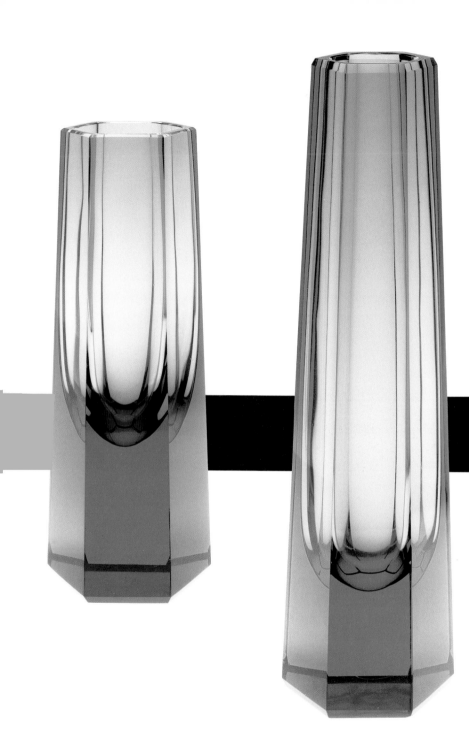

F.L. Wright/Glasfabriek Leerdam, *hexagonal vase and proportionally reduced model,*
1928-1929, cut emerald-green crystal, height 30 and 42 cm

The cooperation between the Glasfabriek Leerdam and the world-famous architect Frank Lloyd Wright was for many years known only to specialists. A vase, an incomplete correspondence and a few drawings were the silent witnesses of this. A number of recent publications and the sudden emergence of two unknown models were the pretext for a new and more detailed study of this Dutch-American collaboration. Archival research has unearthed so much new material that the history of this product is now one of the best-documented histories of the development of a pre-war product. Usually only written source material is preserved. In this exceptional case we also have access to the verbal agreements between the client and the designer. These are annotated in a diary of P.M. Cochius, the director of the Glasfabriek Leerdam, which he kept during a long journey through the United States. In the meantime the more-or-less complete correspondence has been found, as well as more than sixty drawings of a complete, very extensive breakfast and drinks services and other items such as candelabra and various vases.

In the literature about the Glasfabriek Leerdam the emphasis is invariably placed on the production of the art glass collection, which was contributed to by numerous outstanding artists, designers and architects such as K.P.C. de Bazel, H.P. Berlage, Cornelis de Lorm, Chris Lebeau and of course A.D. Copier, the factory's resident designer. Their designs became synonymous with avant-garde Dutch design. The factory worked on a much smaller scale with foreign designers. That the factory relied to a far greater extent for its income on the production of building materials, bottles, jars and everyday glassware for export is less well known. At that time America was an important customer for vast quantities of richly decorated utilitarian glass, the design of which ran entirely counter to the high artistic pretensions of the directorate and the artists. In order to promote the overseas export of art glass, utility glass and building materials such as bricks and 'graniver' mosaic tiles, the factory undertook various promotional activities. Much energy was spent on showrooms throughout the United States, a network of representatives and the design of products that would appeal to the tastes of the American market. It even seems that there was serious talk of the establishment of production facilities in America, staffed by glassblowers from Leerdam. The trump card of all these plans was the collaboration with the architect Frank Lloyd Wright. During a study trip to America Cochius was regularly focused.

'It is little wonder that, here in America, he is the great man who, notwithstanding all the opposition that he encounters, is still regarded as the man. Otto Kahn, the best-known architect of skyscrapers in N.Y. said: 'We are the businessmen but Frank is the genius'. We may therefore be rightly proud that he has now declared himself ready to work exclusively through and for us, not only for table glass but also for glass building materials.'

P.M. Cochius, travel diary, 1928, United Glassworks, Schiedam,
with thanks to Johan Soetens

Until recently it was assumed that Berlage provided the stimulus for approaching Wright. From the recently discovered archival material it appears that it was P.M. Cochius himself who sought contact with the American architect in 1922 via Berlage.

'Highly esteemed Mr Berlage,
I would be glad to come into contact with Mr Frank Lloyd Wright, about whom you have written in the last edition of "Wendingen", with the aim of requesting him to design glass for us for America. May I accordingly ask if you would be willing to provide us with an introduction to the aforementioned gentleman?'

Letter from P.M. Cochius to H.P. Berlage, dated 4 October 1922,
Collection Netherlands Architecture Institute, Rotterdam

Berlage, who had visited America and who was familiar with Wright's work, had unfortunately never met him. His letter of recommendation, together with a letter of introduction from Cochius never reached Wright because, unbeknownst to Berlage, he had re-housed. It was not until 1927 that contact was finally made via Mr M Das, Leerdam's American representative. The interest in making renewed attempts to contact Frank Lloyd Wright were undoubtedly reawakened by the publication in 1926 of a series of six issues of *Wendingen* devoted to his work. There followed an intensive correspondence between Cochius and Wright. To give greater impetus to the project, Cochius paid Wright a number of visits at his house in Taliesin during his business trip to America in the spring of 1928. Within a short period negotiations were made, plans developed, drawings produced, contracts signed and production schedules fixed. All agreements were noted in the finest detail in Cochius' diary and later in letters. Back in the Netherlands, communications by post and telegram, and the shipments of proof models caused such delays for the entire process that nothing more came of the planned production for more than sixty

The diary that Cochius kept during his American trip contains many interesting bits of information. So, on 20 November 1928 he wrote: '*Has designed a vase 14" high round & triangular. Can be made smaller in proportions.*'

A day later: '*This morning Mr L.W. completed his first drawings; three vases triangular, octagonal* [this turned out to be hexagonal] *and round, blown, and so easily pressed, reducible to various dimensions. The pressing with seams in the middle, in primitive glass: Preferably in white glass or 3/4 crystal. In America there are no good vases. L.W. will draw others: he finds those that we have made until now in Holland extremely beautiful. He is absolutely of the opinion that the American market is going in a different direction. For A.* [America] *the vases will have to be larger. Less refined, more primitive. The pressed ones may show their seams, although there is no stated objection to polishing off the seams a little that the glass shows pressing faults. The colour must be really good.*'

P.M. Cochius' travel diary, 1928

designs for a complete dinner and drinks service, various candlesticks and vases, two sculptures and various building materials than a handful of maquettes for vases and a glass brick. An important factor in the failure of the project was the unproducibility of many of the designs. Furthermore, the growing economic recession did little for Leerdam's market position in America, securing the final nail in the coffin of the collaboration.

As far as is known the company produced two different models. The best known is the six-sided vase, produced in two sizes. Of the largest size four examples are known. Of the smallest size there is only a single example known.

Cochius and Wright conducted an exhaustive correspondence about the production of the design. Wright never approved the example for production. He found that the interior and the exterior did not match each other. Therefore he suggested a relief for the interior, something that was technically impossible.

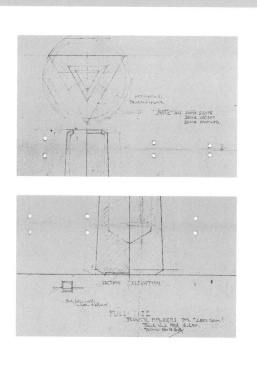

We are ready now with the manufacture of one of your vases and are sending you a copy for your judgement.

Letter from Cochius to Wright, 15 April 1929

The glass vase duely arrived. [...]

It is a beautiful piece of glass and, made as you made it, must have cost a lot of money. To my mind, however, the cut surface and the irregular blown interior make a lively discord. I had anticipated the lines of the interior being similar to the exterior, not yet being familiar with the process of manufacture.

Now this vase, however, has given me an idea which may work out into something. The idea is, interior pattern contrasting and harmonizing with the exterior form. Take this vase with the narrow top and the wide bottom — leave it open at the bottom, say, and design for the interior walls a core that make contrasting rectilinear pattern. This interior pattern might be quite decorative in effect so that when refraction the light from within, it would work harmoniously with the reflected light on the outside. The opening at the bottom could then be plugged or sealed and ground off (the mark or seal being cast in it).

Apparently you made this vase with a round-exterior and cut down the sides. But if the vase were to be pressed in a mould there would be some standing seams on the edges to be ground off later and I should think it might save a great deal of work.

Could we not develop a mould-technique so that we might be able to press the vase to get not only the exterior but also the interior form say over a core with modelled sides which core could later be removed through the wide opening left at the bottom. Then grinding and setting a glass plug or stopper at the bottom. That stopper of glass could be easily made sufficiently water-tight. This process of making interior pattern would open me a number of possibilities in architectural form that I could work out in very interesting phases.

Letter from Wright to Cochius, 16 May 1929

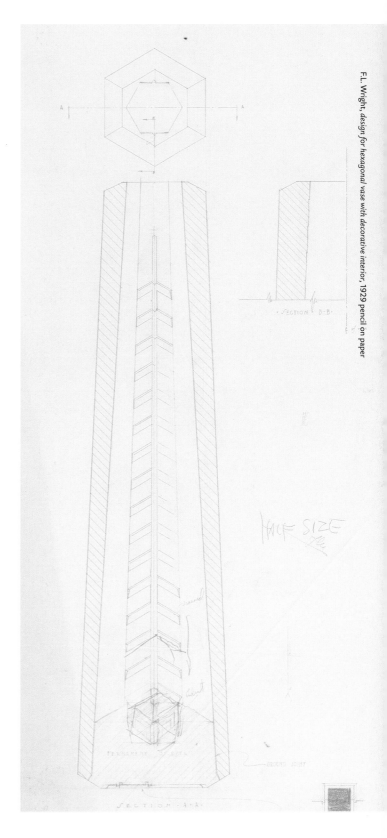

F.L. Wright, *design for hexagonal vase with decorative interior*, 1929 pencil on paper

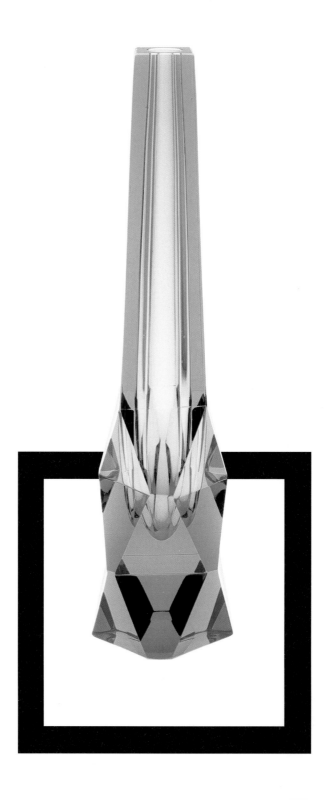

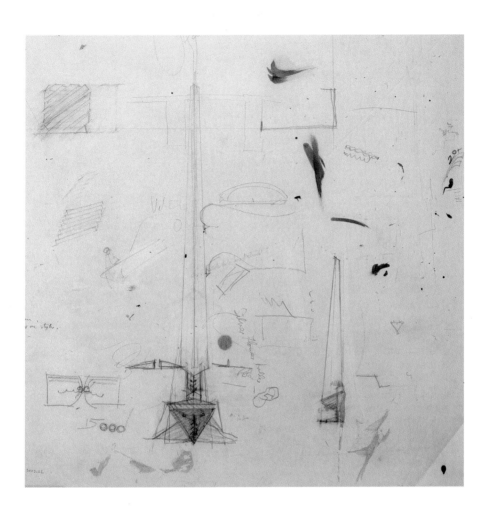

Until recently the production of the so-called 'budvase' was unknown. This obelisk-shaped vase, intended for a bud, rested on a pyramid-shaped foot. A sketch specially adapted by Wright shows a zigzag pattern on the foot, which can be found on the base of the final vase.

literature

J. Ambaum, 'Ontwerpen van Frank Lloyd Wright voor de glasfabriek Leerdam', *Jong Holland*, 1, 1984, pp. 35-51

Thimo te Duits, *Geperst glas uit Leerdam*, Assen/Leerdam 1991, pp. 97-100

Thimo te Duits, 'Twee vazen (prototypes)', *Bulletin van de Vereniging Rembrandt*, vol. 3 (autumn 2002) no. 3, pp. 22-24

The purpose of every stylistic period is not to come up with variations of form, but rather to find the true and only possible solution for construction and manufacture; a balanced whole in which the practical requirements of a practicable construction are solved in an economical fashion.

Rietveld, *The Chair*, 1930

Zigzag Chair circa 1932

Gerrit Rietveld (1888-1964)

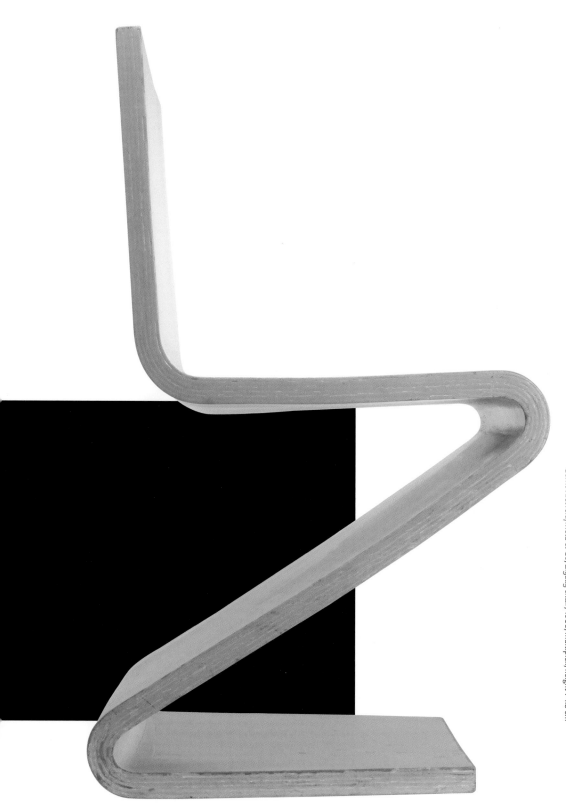

Gerrit Rietveld/Metz & Co, *Zigzag chair*, 1938, multiplex, height 74.8 cm

If one had to sum up Gerrit Rietveld's oeuvre in a single word, 'reductionism' would probably be the most appropriate term. However, this does not tell us a great deal because reduction is also one of the most important themes – possibly even the most important theme – of the entire history of twentieth-century art, architecture and design. In contrast to many of his contemporaries, such as Ludwig Mies van der Rohe, Rietveld strove not so much for an aesthetic effect, but more for a practical object. By returning furniture to its essential, preferably standardised, components, Rietveld wanted to create the possibility for affordable industrial production.

In the famous Red-Blue Chair designed around 1918 – at that time still devoid of

The writer Paul Overy has spoken of a, 'parody or pastiche, in which Rietveld achieves the apparently impossible by constructing a cantilevered chair out of what would appear to be the least appropriate material.'

colour – Rietveld already placed the emphasis very clearly on construction and economy of materials. Although he had already made a great step in the direction of mechanised production with this 'undressed' chair, Rietveld continued to search for new possibilities in this area during the 1920s. Around 1927 this resulted in a number of experimental models, made from a single sheet of fibreboard or triplex, including the so-called 'Birza' chair. Despite the fact that Rietveld realised his ideal of a 'single-piece' chair with this model, in practice the chair was difficult to fabricate and the production remained restricted to two examples.

Nonetheless, the Birza chair can be considered as the forerunner of one of Rietveld's most successful designs – the Zigzag chair. As with the above-mentioned design, it was Rietveld's intention to make this chair from a single sheet of material, which is clearly visible in the earliest prototype of the Zigzag. This chair, made around 1932, consists of a steel frame over which a sheet of fibreboard is folded and fastened with small screws. However, the fibreboard split along the frame's sharp edges and Rietveld was forced to use a more conventional construction. In another prototype, presumably made a little later, Rietveld replaced the fibreboard with four sheets of multiplex, mounted on a similar frame.

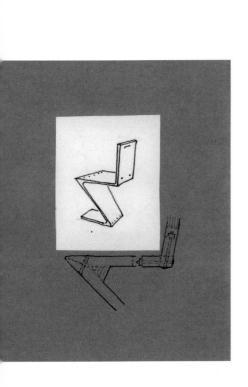

In the final design he did away with the frame altogether. The chair now consisted only of four joined slightly tapered planks. The backrest and seat were joined by means of a glued dovetail joint, while nuts and bolts were used for the two oblique angles. To give the construction the necessary strength these two 45° angles were supported by a thin wedge.

With its floating character, this chair is conceptually strongly allied to the cantilevered tubular steel chairs that were produced in various forms from the mid-1920s onwards. In 1932 Rietveld too created such a tubular steel chair that is remarkable for its diagonal emphasis. Nonetheless he chose to produce the Zigzag chair in the less obvious material – namely wood. In this sense, the Zigzag chair can be viewed as a reaction to the mass-produced tubular steel furniture of the period.

Rietveld himself called it,
'not a chair but a designer joke.'

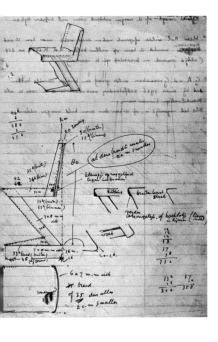

Gerrit Rietveld, page with sketches for the Zigzag chair of folded sections, undated, pencil and ink on paper, 27 x 20 cm / Gerrit Rietveld, *Zigzag chair*, 1934, painted wood, height 75.2 cm

Based on the original model, Rietveld produced numerous variants during the 1930s and 1940s with variations not only in materials, but also of construction, dimensions and finishes. On a design drawing Rietveld described the type of wood to be used as, 'one inch deal cupboard planks from Bruynzeel of Zaandam', whilst over the years it was made of many other sorts of wood including oak and elm. In some examples the joint between the seat and the backrest was strengthened with nuts and bolts.

On the basis of the varying dimensions, three sorts of Zigzag chairs can be distinguished. These include the above-mentioned dining chair with a seat height of approximately 43 cm, that was produced by Rietveld's permanent furniture maker Van de Groenekan as well as the firm Metz & Co, and which is now made by the Italian company Cassina. In addition there were somewhat lower and broader easy-chairs and a smaller category of children's chairs with a much smaller seat.

The Zigzag chair is intended to take up as little space as possible within a room. In order to emphasise this aspect Rietveld sometimes bored circular holes, with a diameter of four centimetres or so, in the backrest of the chair. Although these holes serve little purpose in reducing the chair's weight, they add substantially to

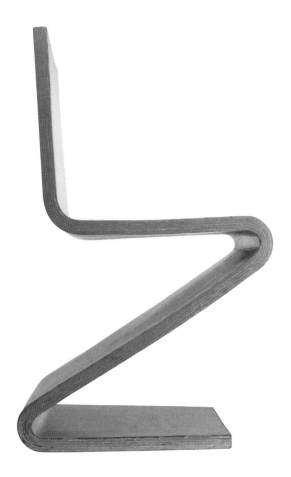

the visual quality of the design. Rietveld added armrests to a few chairs, which were fixed with bolts to the side of the backrest. Usually he also joined the armrest with the leg, thus increasing the strength of the entire construction.

Of all the variants that Rietveld made, there is a single chair – a version in limed multiplex – which most closely approximates the visual ideal of a single-piece chair. Although this chair, which appeared in the Metz & Co catalogue with a price of twenty-five guilders, appears to be constructed of a single sheet, in reality this was not the case. This does not detract from the fact that this chair, with its fluid form, appears to be the model for the single-piece chair with which the Danish designer Verner Panton made his name in the 1960s.

literature

Marijke Küper, Ida van Zijl, *Gerrit Th. Rietveld 1888-1964. Het volledige werk*, Utrecht 1992

Peter Vöge, *The Complete Rietveld Furniture*, Rotterdam 1993

Petra Timmer, *Metz & Co. De creatieve jaren*, Rotterdam 1995

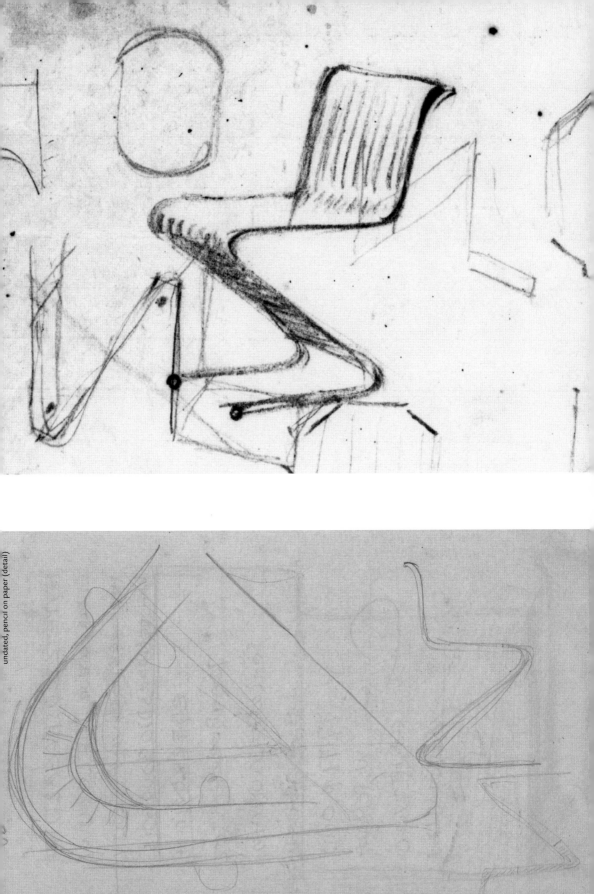

undated, pencil on paper (detail)

Dymaxion Car 1933

R. Buckminster Fuller (1895-1983)

Buckminster Fuller's beliefs and work had not only an idealistic charge but also a political one. He predicted and fought against the dangers of the depletion of materials and fossil fuels. Many called him an optimist. 'Many people say to me that I am an optimist. I always reply that I am absolutely not an optimist, but neither am I a pessimist. I think that optimists and pessimists are unbalanced people. To know that we have options does not make one an optimist. [...] You must understand that I am a very serious realist. I think in terms of responsibility. I cannot risk constructing a building that will fall on people's heads. I thought long and hard before building a dome larger than that of the Pantheon.'

G. Pettena, 'Una vita per ridisegnare il pianeta', *Modo* 10, June 1978, p. 17

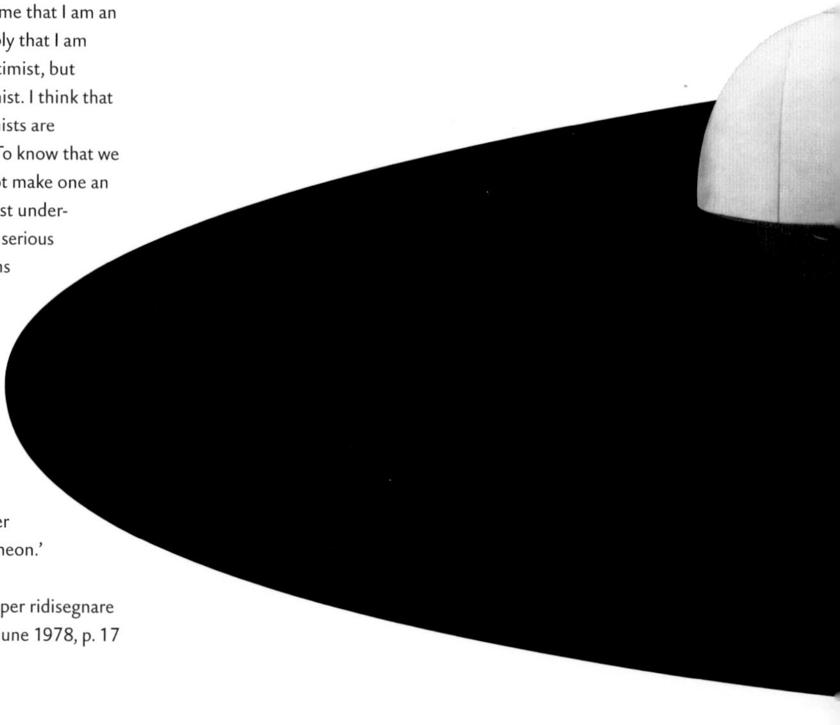

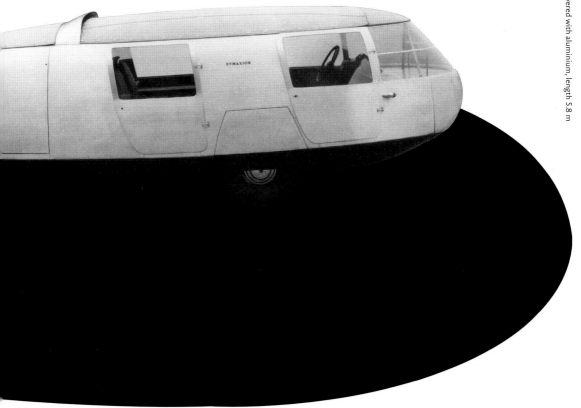

Richard Buckminster Fuller, *Dymaxion Car no.1*, 1933, wooden frame, covered with aluminium, length 5.8 m

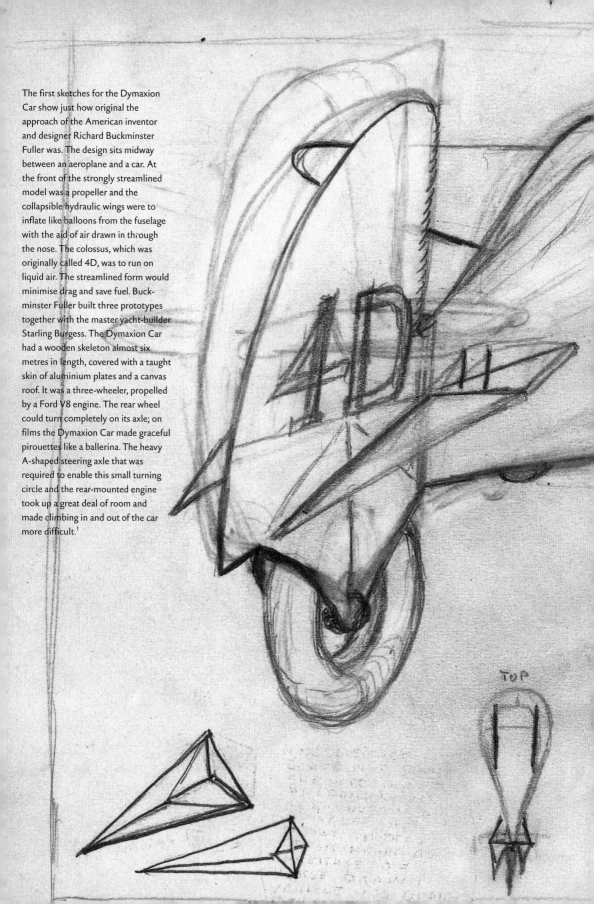

The first sketches for the Dymaxion Car show just how original the approach of the American inventor and designer Richard Buckminster Fuller was. The design sits midway between an aeroplane and a car. At the front of the strongly streamlined model was a propeller and the collapsible hydraulic wings were to inflate like balloons from the fuselage with the aid of air drawn in through the nose. The colossus, which was originally called 4D, was to run on liquid air. The streamlined form would minimise drag and save fuel. Buckminster Fuller built three prototypes together with the master yacht-builder Starling Burgess. The Dymaxion Car had a wooden skeleton almost six metres in length, covered with a taught skin of aluminium plates and a canvas roof. It was a three-wheeler, propelled by a Ford V8 engine. The rear wheel could turn completely on its axle; on films the Dymaxion Car made graceful pirouettes like a ballerina. The heavy A-shaped steering axle that was required to enable this small turning circle and the rear-mounted engine took up a great deal of room and made climbing in and out of the car more difficult.[1]

4D

TRIANGULAR
FRAMED AUTO-AIRPLANE WITH
COLAPSIBLE WINGS - SIMILAR CHILDS
BALOON - INFLATED WITH AIR OR GAS
WHEN RISING IN AIR FROM ROAD .
3 SEPARATE LIQUID AIR TURBINE
CONECTIONS 2 TO EACH OF FRONT
WHEELS AND 1 ONE TO PROPELLER.
PROPELLER LOCKED IN
STATIONERY POSITION
UNTIL ELEVATING.

WINGS ARE
INFLATED RAPIDLY
BY LARGE AIR
INTAKE ON NOSE
OF PLANE THEN
PRESSURE IS
BOOSTED BY
AIR PUMP.

WINGS INFLATED   WINGS

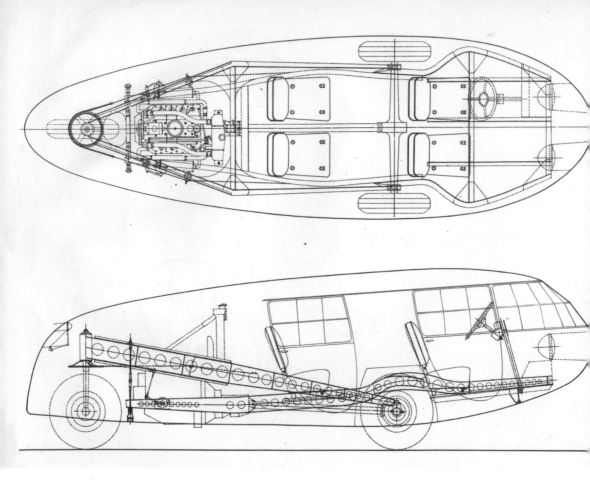

Buckminster Fuller is often described as a twentieth-century Leonardo da Vinci. He was an inventor, philosopher, designer, architect and engineer. As an engineer he was a poet, as a designer he was a philosopher and as a researcher he was an artist. He did not believe in scientific specialisation, because this caused more problems than it solved. His geodesic dome for the American Pavilion at the Montreal World's Fair in 1967 made him world famous. As early as the 1930s he predicted society's development towards a One-Town-World. The need to 'think globally and act locally' was for him always self-evident. Throughout his long life he constantly attempted to develop an 'operating manual' for the management of the planet, which he compared with a spaceship manned by humanity. He developed a contagious holistic vision in which architecture, engineering, geometry, the natural sciences, ecology and anthropology cohered.

Buckminster Fuller developed the Dymaxion concept in the 1920s – a conflation of Dy(namic)-Max(imum)-Ion. Making use of models from the natural sciences he continually attempted to achieve maximum results with the minimum input of materials and energy. He first applied this approach in the Dymaxion House of 1928, followed later by the Dymaxion Car and the Dymaxion Bathroom. He viewed each

ausse,
Lichtenstein,
ur Private
',
Buckminster
er. Design
Kunst einer
senschaft,
ich 1999,
178-201

Buckminster
er,
erating
nual for
ceship
th, Illinois
9

of these designs as mobile units, which could be mass produced by industry. This implied a revolutionary reformation of the construction industry, which despite his passionate commitment and drive was never achieved. The failure of the Dymaxion Bathroom was partly due to resistance from the installation technicians who feared for their livelihood.

Similarly to the architects and artists of the Bauhaus, who used the newest technology in their work, Buckminster Fuller's starting point was always technological. As early as the late 1920s he conducted in-depth research into aviation construction, in which efficient and minimal use of materials was essential to create feather-light aircraft. He borrowed these techniques for his houses, cars and pavilions. The metal Dymaxion House was light enough to be suspended from a single central column, which housed all the services. It was self-supporting and easy to move from place to place. For him design was never a matter of aesthetics, but rather the exploitation of a material's intrinsic qualities within an industrial framework. The aesthetic was a by-product of the chosen materials and construction. He was fond of talking of the transient aesthetic that came about when all superfluous and extraneous factors were eliminated, such as in his aluminium and glass geodesic domes, which appear to float and constantly change colour in the sun.

In total three models of the Dymaxion Car were built. They were in fact sketch models rather than prototypes in the industrial sense, because the design was never put into production. Buckminster Fuller did not pursue the solution of the car's technical problems. Above 80 km/h (50 mph) it went out of control and was unsteerable, an effect that was aggravated by the single rear wheel. The car was also too aerodynamic, further compounding its instability. Today this would be solved with the addition of spoilers, which use airflow to keep the car on the ground, but this principle was not widespread in the 1930s. Above all it seemed that the design was too futuristic, in spite of the public's enthusiastic response. Nonetheless the Dymaxion Car certainly contributed to the subsequent development of the motor car, if only because Buckminster Fuller had little regard for the then current 'horseless carriage' form that dominated car styling.

27 October 1933 the first Dymaxion Car was involved in a serious accident. The French Minister of Aviation and an English aristocrat flew to erica on the Graf Zeppelin to visit the Chicago World's Fair and to try out the Dymaxion Car. During a test-ride, with an experienced driver at the el, they were harassed by a so-called 'sightseer': another car which drove alongside them in order to get a closer look at the futuristic car. Afraid that driver would become distracted and crash, they attempted to lose the interloper, but he came closer and closer until a collision was unavoidable, turning the Dymaxion Car. The driver lost his life, the Englishman was seriously wounded, but survived the accident, and the Frenchman was unhurt. ckminster Fuller tapes, 'Everything I Know')

Dymaxion Car no.1 during one of the test-drives, 1933

DYMAXION
The First Stream Line Car in the World

THE FIRST STREAM LINE CAR IN THE WORLD IS HERE ON ITS TRIAL TRIP FROM BRIDGEPORT, CONNECTICUT PRIOR TO ITS EXHIBITION AT THE CHICAGO WORLD FAIR.

ITS DESIGNERS WILL TAKE PASSENGERS ON A SHORT RIDE AT 50c FOR ADULTS AND 25c FOR CHILDREN FROM 2.30 TO 5.30 P. M.

Friday, July 28
Under the Auspices of the
Damariscotta Mills Library

BISCAY CHARITY FAIR
Bremen, Maine

Joy Bottle circa 1948

G. Kiljan (1891-1968)

In 1946 the Hilversum-based soft drinks manufacturer Jan Koster asked his staff to help devise a name for a new product. The criteria were simple: the name should be short, cheerful and have an international ring to it. It was a certain Mr F.A. Bontje, executive secretary of Koster's company, who suggested the name Joy and so won the promised reward of twenty-five guilders and a wristwatch. In 1946 Koster's firm, founded in 1894 by his father, was, by Dutch standards, a medium-sized soft drinks manufacturer.

Jan Koster's plan in 1946 was to develop a soft drink that could compete with Coca-Cola as well with Hero's popular fruit-flavoured fizzy drinks. Even before the war Jan Koster was convinced that Coca-Cola and Hero were the future. For two years, from 1936 to 1938, Koster had acted as a sales agent for Hero. Koster had noticed how

Hero's soft drinks had been undercutting the sales of his own products. In 1946 it was common knowledge that Coca-Cola and Hero were confronted with an over-whelming demand, which they could scarcely satisfy because sugar was still rationed. No great strategic insight was required to understand that when sugar rationering would come to an end, Coca-Cola and Hero would attract the lion's share of the market. Soft-drinks manufacturers that wanted to stay in the game would therefore need to introduce new products that in terms of brand image and quality were the match for Coca-Cola and Hero.

In retrospect it is clear that Jan Koster understood the market very well: develop your own version of an existing product (Hero fizzy orange); give it an arresting brand name (preferably an English one, to appeal to the youth); commission a modern logo (the designer G. Kiljan chose an italic sans-serif type against a red background); ensure that the name is legally protected (the Joy brand name was registered with the Netherlands Industrial Property Office on 10 June 1949); design

G. Kiljan, Joy models, c.1948, turned wood, height max. 20 cm

a packaging that is immediately recognisable amidst thousands of others (an extremely squat 28cl bottle, also designed by Kiljan); and finally, do not shrink from undertaking the necessary advertising. In short: go for a 'me too' product with a huge profile and leave the competition to invest its time and money in developing a truly innovative product. When, on 8 November 1948, sugar was derationed by the Dutch government, Koster was ready to secure Joy's market position against Coca-Cola and Hero, and even to expand at the cost of other manufacturers. Joy served Koster well for more than twenty years. Unfortunately sales figures and market shares are unknown, but from the fact that a number of variants in flavours and packaging were later introduced we can deduce that Joy was a successful product. In 1958 Joy orange was joined by Joy lemon and a year later by a blackcurrant version. With its eye on supermarket sales, the company launched a slender 75cl bottle and when it became clear that many bar owners found the 28cl bottle too large – customers took too long over a bottle – Koster commissioned a new 20cl version. This final bottle was, in essence, a smaller version of the 75cl family-size bottle. Remarkably enough Kiljan's first 28cl bottle was retained as part of the packaging range. This appears to have been a wise decision because for many customers the Joy brand and Kiljan's peculiar little bottle had become inextricably linked. Moreover, the old bottle was depicted on advertisements, mostly illustrated by Cor van Velsen, which still hung throughout the entire country.

In March 1969 Koster's company was taken over by Heineken, which transferred the Joy brand to its soft drinks subsidiary Vrumona in Bunnik. Because Vrumona's portfolio already contained SiSi, Joy was destined to perform a secondary role as a discount brand. All existing Joy packaging, including Kiljan's characteristic little bottle, was destroyed by Vrumona in 1969.

literature

Merkenblad, vol. 35, no. 4 (April 1946), p. 109; vol. 38, no. 6 (June 1949), p. 694; vol. 38, no. 10 (October 1949), p. 1091

Weekblad voor den handel in gedistilleerd, wijn, bier, etc., vol. 43, no. 6 (15 May 1946), pp. 54-55

Misset's vakblad voor de handel in gedistilleerd, wijn, bier en frisdranken, vol. 57, no. 10 (10 May 1960), pp. 268- 269

Elsevier's Weekblad, 14 May 1960, pp. 57-59

Peter Zwaal, *Frisdranken in Nederland. Een twintigste eeuwse produktgeschiedenis,* Rotterdam 1993

DRU Kettle 1954

Wim Gilles (1923-2002)

Wim Gilles/DRU, various stages of the kettle, 1954

To our not so pleasant surprise it turned out that our beautiful DRU kettle with the lovely handle was the worst of the lot. You couldn't get anything lousier.

Wim Gilles 2002

In 1954 Wim Gilles developed a kettle based on new insights and analysis. Scientific research revealed that DRU's existing kettle had performed very poorly. The story behind the design of this new product was included in a technical encyclopaedia in 1955 as an example of industrial design, for the time a relatively new and unknown specialism in the Netherlands. This text is republished in its entirety on pages 111-115.

literature
Technische Winkler Prins Encyclopedie, part 1, Amsterdam 1955
N. Luning-Prak, *Industriële vormgeving*, Amsterdam 1957

Industrial design

Practical circumstances
With the aim [...] of providing an insight into the factors that may be of importance for industrial design, there follows a summary of the factors considered by a designer in his work on a new kettle. Of course this example has no wider applicability. With another product or material (e.g. aluminium), another client or designer, there would of course have been a different result. The starting point for the design of this kettle was the more general aim of attempting to improve the factory's stove enamel.

The main guideline was the result of research by the Gas Association into the practical effects of aluminium kettles of various base diameters filled to varying levels. The practical effect (the number of litres, multiplied by the rise in temperature, divided by the cubic metres of gas used, multiplied by its calorific value) appeared to be strongly dependent upon the base diameter, as shown in the table below, in which the practical effect is given in percentages for various base diameters (in millimetres):

base diameter	167	180	195	200	206
filled to 0.8 litres	48.2	48.5	50.4	51.0	53.7
filled to capacity	50.9	51.3	51.7	53.2	56.5

Filling a kettle with 0.8 litres of water is the most common practice. It seems that the practical effect with a base diameter less than twenty centimetres must be considered insufficient. The second factor was the influence of the form of the base on the practical effect. A ribbed base would be expected to produce a high practical effect (larger surface area) similar to that of a dome-shaped base. However, optimal heat conduction occurred at the point of contact between the flame and the edge of the kettle. With a ribbed base the contact is repeatedly interrupted and with a dome there is a poor conductive cushion of combusted gas. The third factor for the designer was the discovery that the angular transition from the base to the wall of the kettle can produce strong vortices, which can lead to a relative cooling of the wall.

After further research the designer arrived at a list of factors, a 'cahier des charges', including, amongst others, the following suggestions: content approximately 2.5 litres (advice of the Dutch Household Council); place the handgrip in a 'handy' position in relation to the centre of gravity for filling and emptying (advise of the Gas Association); the handgrip should not protrude beyond the sides; use existing whistle (simplification factory); construction consisting of an upper and a lower half, which can both be pressed in a single action (factory); all welding to be smooth or in a single curved surface, so that it can be mechanically welded (factory); rounded

We took two pans with diameters of 220 mm. We placed them one above the other and attached the handle of a milk pan. It looked just like a Gouda cheese. We put a standard whistle on it. We tested it and to our amazement it performed fantastically well. It was far better than any other kettle. Then I tried to get the handle on the top, so that it would not get hot.

Wim Gilles 2002

edges never less than 3.5 mm (enamel factory); retail price preferably similar to that of existing kettle (sales department).

Hereafter a so-called 'spitting' model was constructed by welding together the lower sections of two milk pans (base diameter 22 cm) and adding a random spout and handgrip. This model had a much greater practical effect than the old production model (factory design, c.1935, base diameter 17.5 cm). However, the volume of water was far greater than that given in the specification. Moreover, the shape was strange and therefore probably unmarketable. Analysis of the shape suggested the desirability of omitting a piece of the body to the left and right of the handgrip, while the spout would need to be tipped forward at a 45° angle for ease of pouring. Following these analyses the designer proceeded to make sketches, in search of a fluid transition between the horizontal diameter, 220 mm, and the 41-mm diameter of the spout, positioned at a 45° angle.

This was achieved as follows: a guide line was drawn at an angle starting in front of the kettle, from which radiating planes were formed at angles up to 45°. A circle was drawn in each of the planes, all meeting the same vertical line at the front, their midpoints forming a parabolic arc. This resulted in a form similar to that of some shells. The rounding of the base is also a parabolic arc. In this way it was possible to achieve a completely consistent flow (better than with a circular arc). The sections of this completely mathematically constructed body are fluid and consistently

concave. Convex (negatively arched) lines were avoided, which was important in relation to the vortices.

From the final sketch a three-dimensional working model was made from sheet steel, with the tilted arcs of the circles as the starting point. The space between the plates was filled and a plaster mould was made to which the spout and handgrip were added later. This was used as the presentation dummy for the sales department and for the technicians to clarify the production drawings. The mouldmakers carried out their work on the basis of these final drawings and prepared the stamping tool for the body. In the first production models the original bakelite grip was temporarily replaced with a hollow enamelled handle because the necessary investment for bakelite was too high. As a test the kettle was fitted with a black base, and although this design had practical as well as aesthetic benefits – according to those consulted – it was considered undesirable for production reasons.

A comparison between the old and new kettles gave the following picture: base diameter enlarged from 17.5 cm to 22 cm and no longer dome-shaped but flat; edges rounded off; reduced height; handgrip surmounting the kettle so that it heats up less and is more practical for filling and pouring. In addition, with the old kettle the flame was barely in contact with the kettle, producing vortices that attracted cooler ambient air, whilst with the new kettle the hottest combusted gases formed a continuous mantle around the kettle, so that they also heated the sides. Further-

114

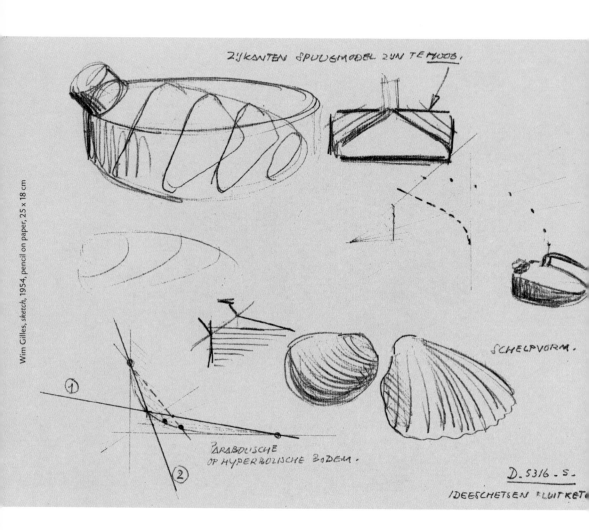

Wim Gilles, *sketch*, 1954, pencil on paper, 25 x 18 cm

ZIJKANTEN SPUUGMODEL ZIJN TE MOOB.

SCHELPVORM.

PARABOLISCHE
OF HYPERBOLISCHE BODEM.

① ②

D. 5316 . S .

IDEESCHETSEN FLUITKETE

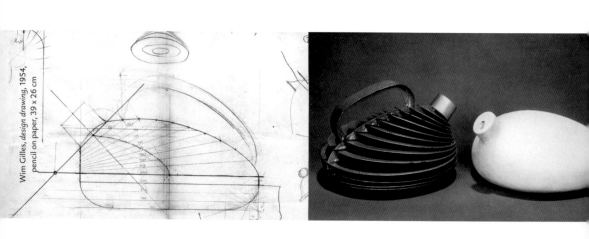

Wim Gilles, *design drawing*, 1954,
pencil on paper, 39 x 26 cm

model, 1994, painted sheet steel and plastic, height 15 cm

more, the cooler ambient air was kept at bay by this hot film of gas. There was also a difference in the space for steam formed at the top of the kettle when filled to capacity. With the old kettle this space was closed off and at boiling point the steam forced the water out through the spout. With the new kettle this space remained open. Another notable feature was that the new kettle (capacity 2.7 litres) appeared no larger than the old kettle (2.5 litres), and the difference in the base diameter was hardly noticeable. Neither did the retail price exceed that of the earlier model.

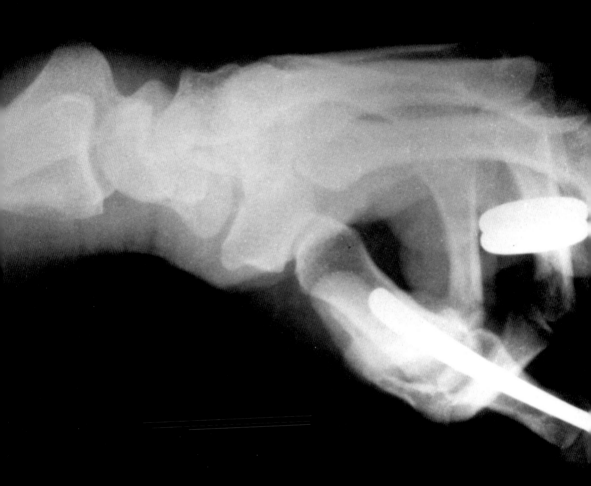

Hopeasiipi 1955

Tapio Wirkkala
(1915-1985)

The silver cutlery Hopeasiipi (Silverwing) from 1955 typifies the work of the Finnish designer Tapio Wirkkala. It was designed in a very functional manner. Wirkkala even took x-ray photographs to see how it lay in the hand. These photographs show clearly that the cutlery is a prothesis of the human body. The streamlined forms, inspired by the bones of birds, are modelled to the human hand and have a visual coherence which fits the malleable character of silver. Function, nature and respect for materials, theses are the three pillars on which Wirkkala's oeuvre is built.

The cutlery was produced by the Finnish silver manufacturers Kultakeskus Oy, which Wirkkala, who already had a reputation for his innovative glass and silver, joined in 1951 with responsibility for modernising its programme. In addition to cutlery for serial production he designed unique coffee services, wedding gifts, church silver and jewellery to order. Wirkkala gave silver a modern image by, for example, combining it with wood and copper. At the Milan Triennale in 1954 these designs received universal admiration.

X-ray of the fork

Tapio Wirkkala/Kultakeskus Oy, Hopeasiipi cutlery, 1955

Already as a child Wirkkala continually carved wooden objects. He was a real go-getter, of whom people said that he had eyes in his fingertips. For him, a new form was born not only from the head but also from the hand. The secret of his success was that Wirkkala worked intensively with craftspeople. Silversmiths, glassblowers and ceramicists taught him to study the techniques and materials thoroughly. He often made a rough sketch or a carved wooden form that the silversmith used to make a model, which they developed together into the finished product. The prototypes for the Hopeasiipi cutlery were also carved in wood.

His inspiration was usually nature. Wirkkala owned a country home in Lapland, where he would spontaneously sketch animals, shells, leaves, ice or reflections of light on water. Sometimes he used these natural forms literally, but usually he abstracted them in combination with geometric forms. In addition to luxury objects he also designed bank notes and bottles for beer, vodka and ketchup. His internship at Raymond Loewy's studio in New York in 1956 made him a real industrial designer. There he learned to work as part of a team on extremely diverse projects and for mass production. Back in Finland he established a studio in 1957, based on Loewy's model, for the Ahlström Group, which owned various companies including the Iittala glassworks. He began to design architecture, interiors and exhibitions for Finnish art and design, which travelled around the world. Wirkkala later set up his own studio working for Finnish clients such as Iittala and Hackmann, but also the Italian company Venini and the

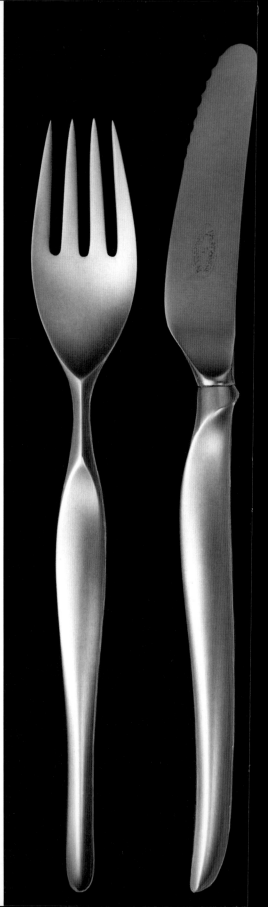

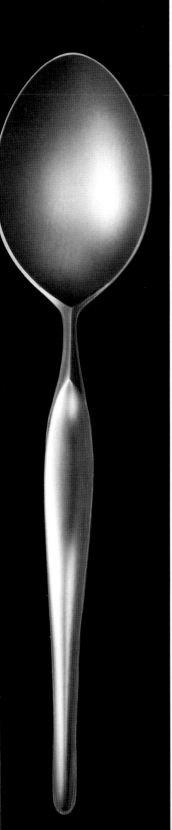

German firm Rosenthal, for who he worked for thirty-three years.

With architects and designers such as Aalto, Franck, Sarpaneva and Nurmesniemi, Wirkkala helped to shape the movement known as Scandinavian Modern, for which Finland received international recognition directly after the Second World War. Influenced by the socialist ideal of beauty for everyone, these designers sought collaboration with industry. They managed to combine elements from Finnish folk culture with industrial production, resulting in objects with powerful forms and bright colours. They managed to temper strict functionalism with their natural, organic forms.

The use of indigenous materials and their working methods were allied to the Bauhaus ideals which came into fashion after the war. Wirkkala: 'All materials have their own unwritten laws... You must never be brutal with the materials you use, and the designer must strive to be in harmony with his materials.' Nonetheless the Hopeasiipi cutlery had a technical flaw, because the fairly angular forms caused the moulds to break too quickly. Because of this it was in production for only a year and thereafter was made only to order. The Tapio cutlery that he designed two years later has been on the market without interruption since 1957.

X-ray of the spoon

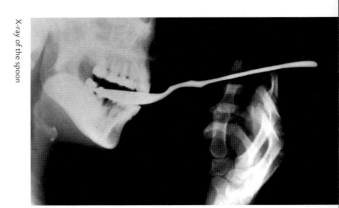

literature
M. Aav (ed.), *Tapio Wirkkala. Eye, Hand and Thought*, Helsinki 2000

PH Kogle Lamp 1958

Poul Henningsen (1894-1967)

Poul Henningsen/Louis Poulsen, *PH Kogle lamp*, 1958, metal, Ø 84 cm

1
Although the lamp was originally called the Pinecone (Kogle), since the 1970s it has mainly been known as the Artichoke, above all in the English-speaking world.

Poul Henningsen was the grand master of light and enlightenment in Danish design. The famous PH lamps are icons, spreading their beautiful yet highly functional glow in homes all over Denmark. The 'Kogle', Pinecone[1], based on a favourite image in Danish forests, is an outstanding example of Henningsen's ultra-modern design vision. Originally designed for the Langelinie Pavilion in 1958, it combines Henningsen's elaborate sense of the festive and the functional in a single design.

The two triple-layered sketch collages that Henningsen made of white and pink acrylic foil, pencil, brown wrapping paper and parchment produce a three-dimensional effect, giving life and tactility to these rather poor materials. The wrapping paper serves as a primitive canvas, an untraditional support from which the motif stand outs with an airy expression. The hand-cut acrylic vitalises the shape of the lamp's shades, which blend in an almost Cubist manner. Like the Dadaist artist Kurt Schwitters, Henningsen used materials from everyday life, ennobling them by shaping them into art. The collages show that, even though Henningsen was a designer who believed in the evolution of technological innovation and who generally used industrially produced materials such as tubular steel, he still conceived his ideas with artistry, avant-garde *esprit* and the deliberation of the handmade.

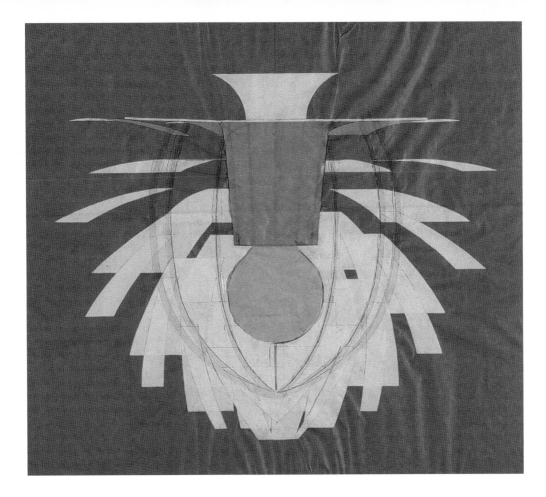

Henningsen passionately considered industrial design as a path to a more rational and modern society inhabited by self-confident and critical citizens. However, the collages create a dialectical encounter between the demanding hand-made design process, requiring concentration and contemplation, and the final dynamic lamp produced in the sterile halls of industry.

His technical and cultural ambitions were those of a radical. He wanted his designs to contribute to the creation of an egalitarian society, but he also believed in the truly humanistic values that could soften the hardness of a totalising machine society. The Pinecone has lighting properties and visual features in common with earlier Henningsen lamps, in particular the visual splendour of Septima, with its seven-shade fitting, and the construction principles of the Globe and the PH5. However, the Pinecone is a true object of luxury, potency and striking organic beauty. His earlier lamps were ringed by speedy, concentric circular shades, but in 1958 he drew upon the international design scene's new sensibility, with its flowing botanical and organic features. He originally intended to create a fixing with seven, free, leaf-like shades symbolising a pinecone.

The design construction was a dream come true for Henningsen and represents a new unity between his rational lighting system and flickering organic lines. The shades were originally made of brushed copper, with a lacquered exterior and a soft pink coating on the interior. The lamp holder and the leaves are held by twelve, polished, nickel-plated armatures and a diagram shows that the armatures are attached to the reflectors as they were in the PH5 and the Louvre. The result is a striking 84 cm-diameter lamp with enormous visual impact. Later smaller versions were made with diameters of 72 cm and 60 cm respectively.

The large version of the Pinecone is designed to take a 500-watt lamp, but Henningsen took no risks with the Langelinie Pavilion, and to ensure the right atmosphere for its spacious interior, he installed a 1000-watt lamp in each fitting. However, when the Pinecone was installed he found that the effect was too strong and decided that a lower wattage could be used. The lamp's impressive presence was enough of a match for the capacious restaurant, creating an appropriate atmosphere of grandeur. The Pinecone was an instant success and in 1968 a new version was introduced with a frosted nickel-coated exterior to the moveable shading leaves. In the mid-1970s the stainless-steel Pinecone shade was born, producing a lamp of pure glamour, and in early 1980 the white Pinecone joined the collection of Poul Henningsen's unique design vision.

information
www.louispoulsen.com

The seven leaves
became ten in the
drawing and twelve in the
Pinecone itself. The
principle is twelve railings
staggered from each
other instead of six
board-fences. The
Pinecone could
therefore be made as a
type of Louvre with six
shades but that gives
more play and richness
and it splits the metal
impression comfortably
with the division into
twelve times six leaves
instead of six rings.

Poul Henningsen, Nyt 1958

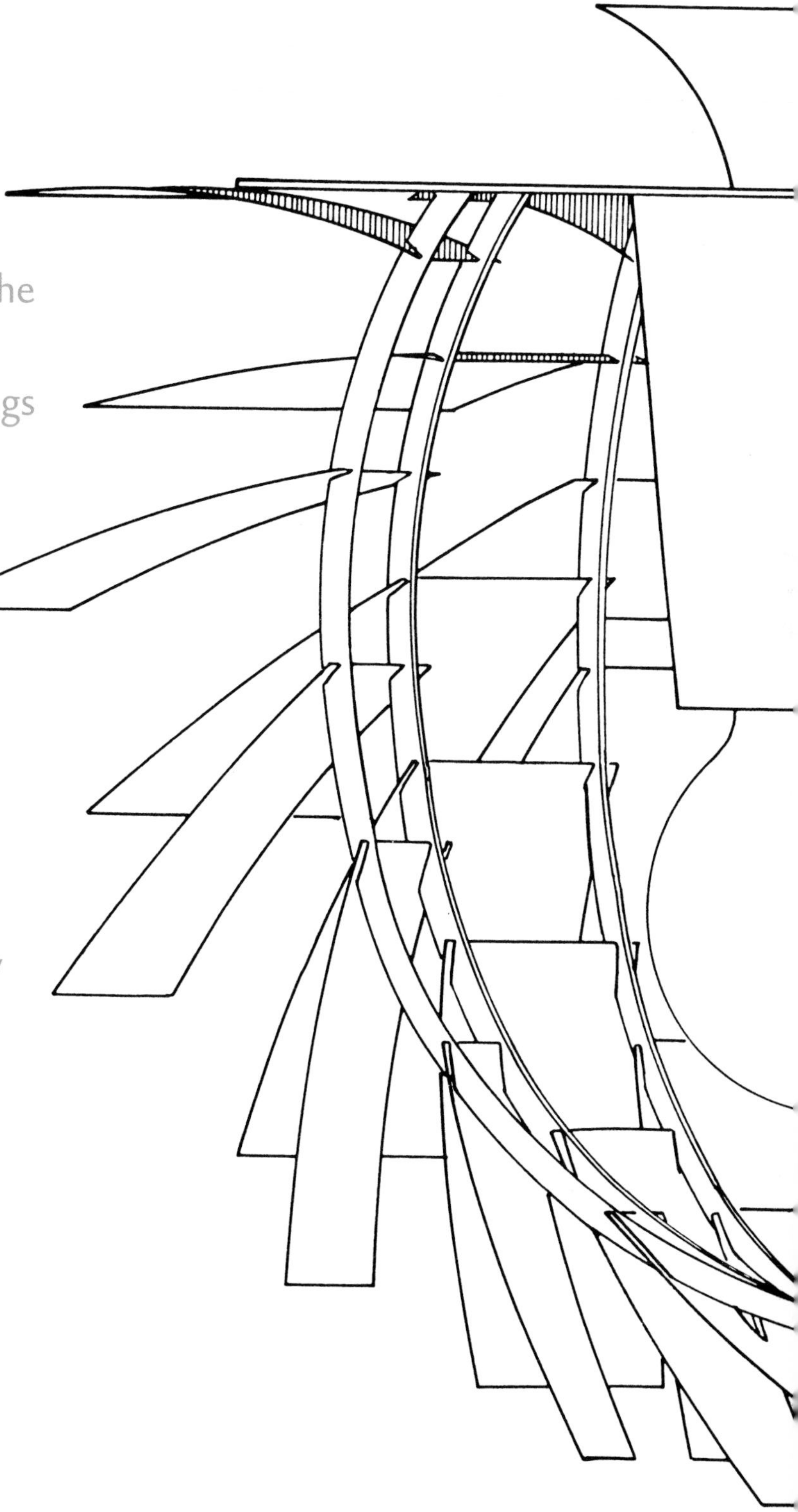

Scooterette 1958-1964

Wim Gilles (1923-2002)

Wim Gilles, Scooterette in folded state, 1964, sheet metal and scooter components, height 80 cm

8-2-1961

Of the surviving drawings this is the
earliest. The sketch concentrates on
the scooterette's construction. The
folding mechanism is clearly visible.
Here the model still has front-wheel
drive.

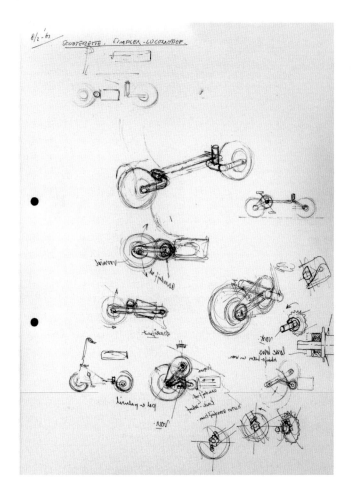

From 1949 to 1953 Wim Gilles worked as a full-time designer for the iron foundry
Diepenbrock & Reigers in Ulft (DRU). Here he developed, amongst other things,
enamelled products for kitchens and bathrooms and coal and gas fires. He also
designed the packaging for these objects. From 1953 he worked as a free-lance
industrial designer for a large number of clients, including his former employer DRU
and the Amsterdam-based bicycle manufacturer Simplex-Locomotief. In 1958 he
was asked to help with the design of various mopeds. At first the commission was
restricted to small, stylistic alterations. There was little room for an industrial
designer because the company was typical of an industry that simply assembles its
products from ready-made components.

Gilles attempted to create more space for himself through a project of his own. Out
of frustration with the inability to store a moped or scooter indoors easily and safely,
he worked on a foldable, space-saving model. Given the lack of space in people's

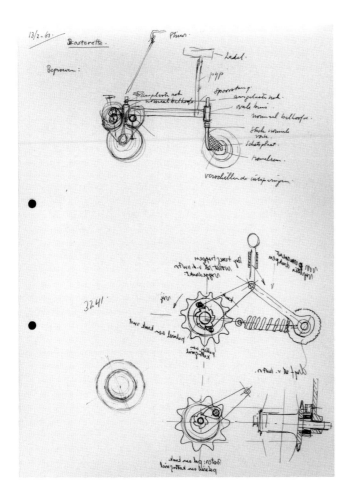

apartments, most people left their mopeds outside, running the risk of theft. Simplex promised to give its material support and Gilles knocked together a working model in his cellar of what was later to be known as the scooterette.

tarted tinkering with a piece of sheet metal and a hammer.

The scooterette was designed to fill a gap in the moped market, which was dominated by the Puch: a noisy machine that could go extremely fast; and the Solex: a bike with front-wheel propulsion, which had a more sleepy image.

The most important principle of the scooterette was a hinged frame. The design is undoubtedly based on the folding bicycle. Gilles worked out the design of his idea on paper for three years. Various drawings document his thought process. In 1960 he showed a miniature model to Simplex and asked if they wanted to buy the idea.

29-12-1961

This sheet contains the first sketches that show the definitive solution of the construction. The motor, explicitly visible for the first time, is in its definitive position above the front wheel. In addition, the chain drive has been moved to the rear wheel. In the shell of the scooterette we can also recognise for the first time the definitive model. The moped's design becomes increasingly clear.

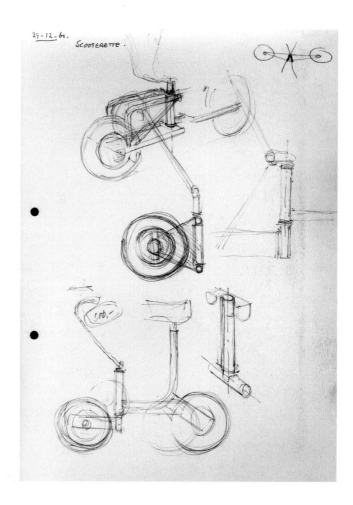

Simplex's agreement enabled Gilles to work up the idea into measured drawings and a functioning prototype. He quickly came up against a variety of problems, which were already familiar to him from existing mopeds. One of these was that the moped and in particular the handlebars had to be independent from the vibrating motor.

The engine had to be completely sprung. Gilles wanted the scooterette to come under the legislation for mopeds. For this to be possible the scooterette would have to have pedals, which drive one of the wheels via a chain, thus activating the motor. Gilles chose to couple the drive mechanism with the front wheel, following the idea that a small motorbike must have weight over its rear wheel in order to provide good road-holding. If the motor was placed at the rear, you would run the risk that, 'if you weren't careful, the whole thing would take off from under your arse.' Although the first sketches show the attempts to fit the transmission to the front-wheel, later the decision was made to link the pedals to the rear wheel. Eventually the pedals no longer played a role in activating the motor. Gilles assumed that the simple inclusion of pedals would be sufficient to pass the moped inspection.

Gilles tested the final prototype himself for a long period. From his house in Bergeijk he rode it for a whole term to the Academy for Industrial Design in Eindhoven where he taught.

From Gilles' correspondence with Simplex it is obvious that he believed steadfastly in the scooterette. He considered that the time was ripe for a radical change in the moped market. According to him, the public had great purchasing power at that time and would not dismiss something totally new. In the scooterette Gilles saw a moped that satisfied in every respect the requirements of the time, something that could not be said of the existing mopeds. That the scooterette got no further than a prototype can be attributed to two factors. Firstly, at the beginning of the 1960s when the scooterette was, in principle, ready for production Simplex had serious financial problems. They simply could not afford to take the risks associated with a new product. Secondly, the legislation governing mopeds changed in this period. According to Simplex the scooterette's small wheels defined it as a 'motorbike', which meant that the rider would be required to have a licence and to pay road tax. The latter was the main argument against the further development of the scooterette.

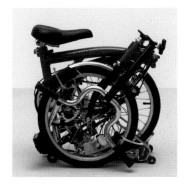 

The folding principle of Gilles' scooterette displays striking similarities with Julian Vereker's and Adrew Ritchie's Brompton folding bicycle of 1978, that collapses to an extremely handy and minimal volume. Their design was put into production by Brompton Bicycle Ltd in 1986. It is the smallest folding bicycle with the best riding characteristics.

21-5-1962

This sheet shows sketches that develop the positioning of the motor on the front wheel. Gilles sought the best way of mounting the motor to the frame. A notable detail is the excellent shock absorption.

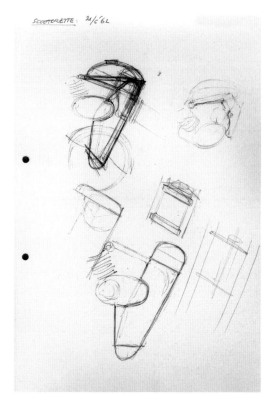

1963

The first complete design sketch of the scooterette. We see the scooterette obliquely from the front. Above this design are two smaller drawings of the scooterette, in its folded and unfolded states. The saddle folds forward at a 90° angle, so that it ends up under the frame. To give the folded scooterette stability, the rear wheel rests on the extended luggage rack, to which rubber supports have been added. The front section of the scooterette, with the motor above the front wheel, is the only part that is non-collapsible. The sketches are very precise and display a striking resemblance to the definitive prototype. However, in the drawing the handlebars fold downwards to the right, whereas in the prototype they fold back at a 90° angle.

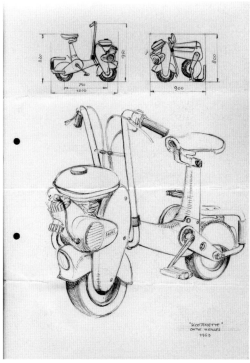

Shell Logo
1967-1971

Raymond Loewy
(1893-1986)

Compagnie de l'Esthétique Industrielle, Parijs

The brand name Shell was introduced towards the end of the nineteenth century by the London-based firm Samuel & Co. This company originally traded in antiques, curiosities and decorative shells from the Far East, which were very popular in England at the time. From the 1890s the company increasingly focused on the fast-growing trade in oil. This shift in activities required a new trading name. Ironically enough the new name used by the company from 1897 onwards – Shell Transport and Trading Company – was based not on the product that would make the company's fortune, but on the less profitable trade in shells.

From the turn of the century the company's name was accompanied by the image of a shell. The original choice of a mussel shell was changed in 1940 for that of a scallop. In varying forms this type of shell has remained the company's trademark to this day.

The shell acquired its red and yellow colouring only in 1915 when the company opened its first service stations in California. Within this strongly competitive market immediate recognition was a prerequisite. The primary colours red and yellow fulfilled not only this requirement, but also referred at a secondary level to the colours of the Spanish flag, with which many of California's inhabitants felt a strong bond.

Despite his technical education, Loewy worked for a number of years as a fashion illustrator before opening his own design studio in 1929. Commissions swiftly began to flood in. Paradoxically enough, during the crisis Loewy swam with the tide. The manufacturers that had survived the great crash were confronted with the bitter necessity of stimulating consumer interest in one way or another. Within this stagnant market it seemed that progressive design was an effective means of trumping the competition.

Between two products equal in price, function and quality, the better looking will outsell the other.

Loewy was certainly not the only representative of the professionalisation of design. From the end of the 1920s a large number of American designers – mostly trained as advertising artists or set designers – opened their own studios. These included Walter Dorwin Teague (1883-1960) and Henry Dreyfuss (1904-1972) who, much like Loewy, managed to gain a large number of clients within a short period. Although nearly all American designers of the 1930s employed a similar stream-lined language of form based on aerodynamics, they put different accents on their approach to design problems. Teague had a fairly deterministic vision, within which the designer's task was to invest the product with perfect form. Dreyfuss' starting point was a particular interest in all aspects relating to the ergonomics of a product. Whereas for Teague and Dreyfuss aesthetics and utility were respectively central Loewy held the opinion that the largest target audience was the best.

One should design for the advantage of the largest mass of people, first and always.

Not least in importance for his clients, he aimed himself explicitly at the lowest common denominator. To realistically appeal to the broadest possible audience Loewy designed his products according to his self-coined principle MAYA (Most Advanced Yet Acceptable). By this he meant that in order to satisfy the tastes of the largest public a product should be innovative, but certainly not too revolutionary. When Loewy was asked by Shell to design its house style in 1967, he was already responsible for many world-famous designs and led one of the world's largest design studios with offices in the United States and Europe. That Loewy entrusted this million-dollar contract to the Compagnie de l'Esthétique Industrielle (CEI), as his Paris office was called, was obvious. Shell was a European client and the CEI had already successfully taken care of the house styles of companies such as Spar, Co-op and BP.

With the design of logos Loewy strove increasingly for mass recognition.

am looking for a very high index of visual memory retention. other words, we want anyone who has seen the logotype, even eetingly, to never forget it, or at least forget 'slowly'.

Viewed from this standpoint, the logo that served Shell in the 1960s left rather a lot to be desired. Seen in low light or from a distance the logo was pushed into the background by the company's name. Loewy decided to carry out a number of necessary changes. In the first place, the company name was detached from the logo and placed – in a new, more contemporary typeface – against a white background. In some instances the company name was eradicated entirely and the shell functioned independently. The shell itself was also subject to changes. Whereas since 1904 the logo consisted of a more or less naturalistic depiction of a scallop shell, Loewy now designed a brand-mark that was reduced to the most elementary characteristics of this kind of shell: a rectangular base, a rounded upper half and radiating ribs. In addition, the original red background was replaced with a broad red band, which outlined the stylised shell. Finally the colours were adjusted slightly – somewhat brighter shades were chosen for both the red and the yellow, by which the contrast was increased.

A logo is an important part of a house style, but certainly not the only one. As such Loewy's team did not restrict their attention only to Shell's trade mark. They also designed new packaging for products, new colour schemes for the company's lorries and even new clothing for Shell's employees. In addition the CEI developed, following the MAYA principle, a modular architectonic concept for the set up of petrol stations, whereby the petrol sales could be increased and the level of service improved.

literature
Raymond Loewy, *Industrial Design*, Amsterdam 1979
Angela Schönberger (ed.), *Raymond Loewy. Pioneer of American Industrial Design*, Munich 1990
Per Mollerup, *Marks of Excellence. The History and Taxonomy of Trademarks*, London 1999
Michael Johnson, *A Problem Solved. A Primer in Design and Communication*, London 2002

WK Chair
(model 275)
1956-1965

Panton Chair
1957-1960

Verner Panton
(1926-1998)

Verner Panton (with glasses), Rolf Fehlbaum and Manfred Diebold with the mould for the Panton Chair, c. 1966

Verner Panton was the black sheep of twentieth-century Danish design. He stood apart from conventional furniture design and its focus on the simple, the logical and the use of natural materials. Instead Panton scandalised this functionalist doctrine and modernist puritanism with his outré plastic chairs and his psychedelic interior designs. Floating on an unbridled design imagination, full of adventure, magic and innovations he expressed new ultra-modern attitudes in synthetic, colour-infused creations full of spunk and funk. The Panton Chair from 1959-1960 is just such an enigmatic object, a curvaceous, posing supermodel of a chair, which created a world-wide sensation: the world's first single-piece injection-moulded plastic chair, pushing plastic's potential into a new orbit. The extravagant, sculptural qualities of this futuristic monochrome stackable chair have made it a modern classic.

Verner Panton had envisioned the creation a chair constructed from a single piece of material since the 1950s. In 1956 he submitted a stackable, cantilevered dining chair, with a base, seat and back made from a single material, to the European Competition for Furniture Design organised by the WK Group (Neue Gemeinschaft für Wohnkultur). As he noted in the competition drawing, the material could be either transparent/compact plastic or a plastic-coated wooden laminate. Panton

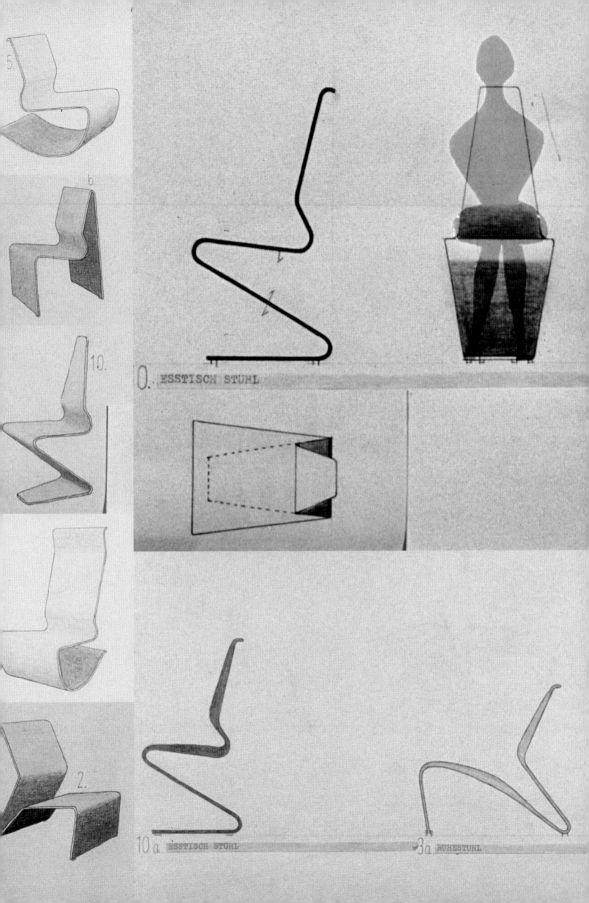

0. ESSTISCH STUHL

10 a ESSTISCH STUHL   3 a RUHESTUHL

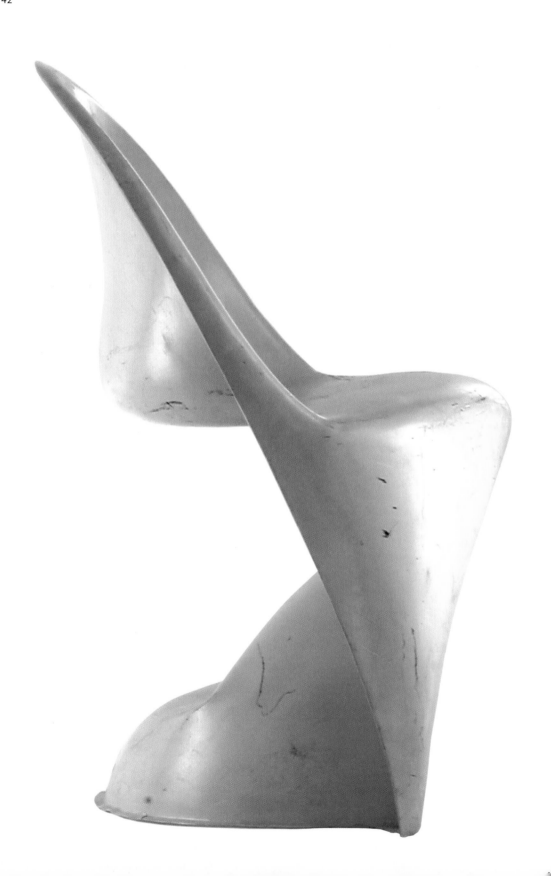

did not win a prize, however, the moulded plywood WK Chair, later manufactured by Thonet in 1965, signalled what was to be expected from the unorthodox Danish designer in the years to come. It foreshadows the future essence of the Panton Chair with its S-shaped form, and has certain formal parallels with Gerrit Rietveld's Zigzag Chair from 1932. The notion of a single-piece chair continued to fascinate Panton and the possibility of realising his dream turned out to be near at hand by the end of the 1950s. The progressive development of extremely flexible plastics was the answer to his prayer. Several sketches made by Panton between 1957 and 1960 indicate the basic structure of the Panton Chair. The drawings reveal an impatient mind, with repetitive scribbled motifs in red ink and pencil in two layers. The flat base of the WK Chair is replaced by the vault-like base of the future Panton Chair and the sculptural form of the seat and back is transformed into a more ergonomically moulded seat shell. From these sketches emerged the preliminary version of the Panton Chair manufactured in 1960 by Dansk Akryl Teknik using polyester. The expressiveness of line has similarities with the final Panton Chair, but it lacks the dynamic *esprit* and harmonious union between the individual elements and the whole. Still this chair was an important step on the journey towards the definitive

Verner Panton, sketches for the *Panton Chair*, c. 1960, coloured pencils on paper (detail)

Panton Chair that we know today. He travelled all over Europe looking for a manufacturing partner and in 1963 he met Willi Fehlbaum, the Basel-based manufacturer who produced furniture under license for the Herman Miller Collection. However, the American company expressed some reservations concerning the mass production of the chair, and it was not until the younger Rolf Fehlbaum contacted Vitra's Development Division that the design process was given real impetus. In close collaboration with Herman Miller and Vitra, Panton produced ten further prototypes made of hand-laminated, fibreglass-reinforced polyester. He harmonised the formal ideals with plastic's natural potential and the technical conditions of manufacturing and thus created an object with a physical expressiveness and almost sexual desire. The Panton Chair was finally produced by Vitra in 1967 under the Herman Miller Label. It was presented in a limited edition of 100-150 pieces using cold-pressed fibreglass-reinforced polyester. Herman Miller states that it was thereafter made from 'Baydur', an HR polyurethane-foam produced by the Bayer Leverkusen company, and came in seven colours. It was the first product developed jointly by Vitra and Bayer Leverkusen to be included in the Herman Miller collection. Vitra switched to a more economical thermoplast injection moulding in 1970 and continued production until 1979, when the license was returned to Verner Panton. In 1983 Horn GmbH & Co. KG in Rudersberg produced the chairs, and it has once again been made by Vitra since 1990. Towards the end of the 1990s Vitra introduced a new and definitive, authorised version of the chair. It is made of injection-moulded polypropylene and was launched in 1999 as a less expensive version. Polypropylene shares formal qualities with the initial use of polystyrene, but the obvious difference is the matt surface compared with the high gloss of the original model, thus turning the Panton Chair into a 'cooler' product.

The story behind the chair reveals Verner Panton's nature as a design wizard. He combined a childlike curiosity with technological knowledge and the scrutinising mind of a researcher. He is rightly acknowledged as the ultimate Pop designer, matching the new era of playfulness, unconventional lifestyle and aspiring con-sumerism. But there is also an aspect of surrealism to his universe, questioning the belief in rationalism as the key to harmony and happiness. He believed in the sub-conscious as an ongoing revolution, releasing the mind and body from a mecha-nised society based on rationalism and a limiting hegemony. He overcame the dichotomies of high and low culture, combining them into a new territory, where one can experience a free-spirited physical haven amongst 'living towers', flying furniture and space-like installations in technicolour. Verner Panton's design sphere is a slit in time, that allows a glimpse of true recognition, where the past, present and future former melt into a single existence.

literature
Exh.cat., *Verner Panton, the Collected Works*, Weil am Rhein (Vitra Design Museum) 2000

New Alphabet 1961-1967

Wim Crouwel (1928)

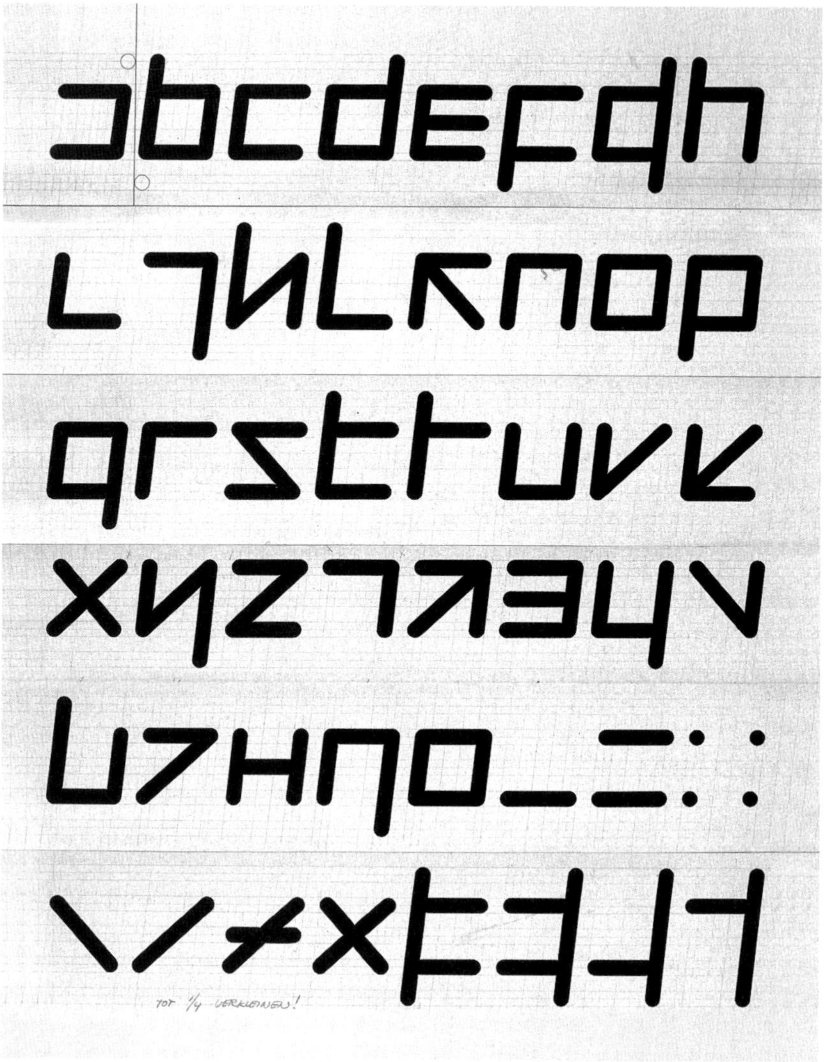
tot 1/4 verkleinen!

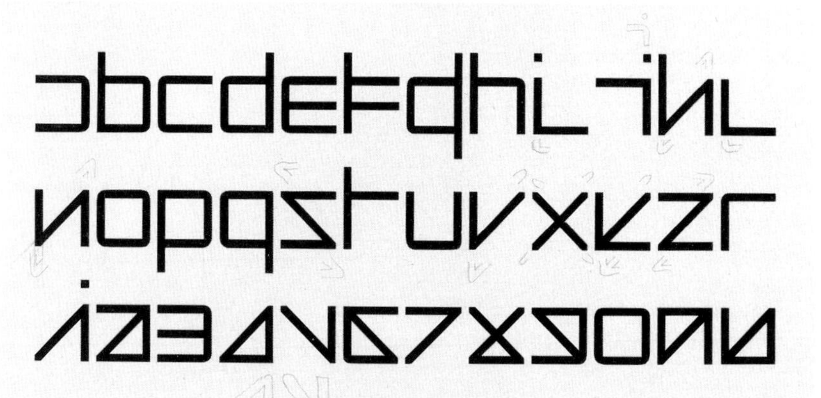

Wim Crouwel, New Alphabet, proof, July 1964, pencil and ink on tracing paper

Throughout the course of history alphabets have developed along two main lines: 'architectography' and 'calligraphy'. These are characterised by their different use of writing tools and the surfaces used and by the different speeds of the writing process. Architectography engendered the upper case alphabet, with letters of the same height, fitting between two parallel lines and without ascenders and descenders. By contrast, calligraphy gave rise to the lower case alphabet, with letters of varying lengths, drawn both between two parallel horizontal lines and with protruding strokes, tails and signs.

During the twentieth century a special family of typefaces was designed, the so-called 'mono-alphabets', which do not contain the usual doubling of signs for a single sound (a and A, b and B), but have exclusively upper case or lower case letters. The origins of these attempts to bring letters back to a 'minimal working form' probably stem from the Dutch influence on German design thinking. For example the work of Peter Behrens was strongly influenced from 1904 onwards by the designs of

J.L.M. Lauweriks. This Dutch architect and theosopher played a key role in geo-metrical research, based on the application of a modular grid and simple iterations to architecture, the applied arts and decoration.

In 1917 the magazine *De Stijl* was founded and with it the Neo-plasticist movement, led by Theo van Doesburg. The first cover of *De Stijl* bore a logo, taken from a paint-ing by Vilmos Huszár, in which the words are described by a series of rectangles that force the characters into an elementary structure. In the first issue a number of principles were formulated on this simplified and non-decorative use of forms, which would thereafter come to characterise the Neoplasticist programme. The artistic avant-garde of the 1920s encompassed many different tendencies, from Piet

Wim Crouwel, New Alphabet, proportional grid, c. 1966, ink on paper

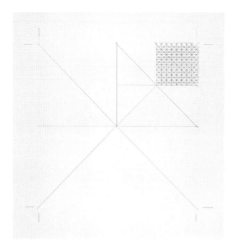

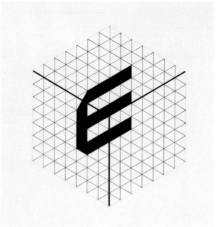

Mondriaan's Neoplasticism and El Lissitzsky's Constructivist utopias to Kurt Schwitter's Dadaist tone poems and Gerrit Rietveld's furniture. In place of 'depiction', the artists of De Stijl employed 'form' as an expression of pure reality. Piet Mondrian's structural abstraction was intended to express 'the intimate construction of reality', freed from any subjective content. In typography, Neoplasticist theories were expressed through the preference for 'linear' letterforms, which were considered more functional, more legible and better suited to standardisation. The emphasis was placed on the structural elements of typography within the orthogonal division of space.

The innovative, avant-garde elements employed in typography came together in the Bauhaus where, in the field of type design, vital research was undertaken into functional, neutral letterforms without embellishments. The most important lettertypes designed at the Bauhaus are fairly representative: the *Stencil* (1925), designed by Josef Albers, features geometric and modular forms based on the combination of elementary, standardised signs. The same can be said of Herbert Bayer's *Universal* (1925), with which he intended to design an international, functional, standardised lettertype with precise forms, which would be easy to understand and to remember. These themes played a role in German culture throughout the 1920s, from Jan Tschichold's mono-alphabet (1926-1929) to the research and tests of László Moholy-Nagy and Joost Schmidt, from Kurt Schwitters' mono-alphabet of 1927 to Paul Renner's experimental lower case letters for the provisional version of *Futura* (1927-1930).

Later developments, from A.M. Cassandre's characteristic *Peignot* (1937) to Max Bill's examples, as fresh today as they were in 1944, from Bradbury Thompson's first *Monoalphabet* (1945), based on *Futura*, and his subsequent *T26* (1950), based on *Baskerville*, can all be seen as attempts to produce – as Max Bill put it: 'a lettertype of word-images, which, through the emphasis on the vowels, can be read with the aid of machines and which is more easily legible for people: a lettertype of our time.'

Wim Crouwel, New Alphabet, proof with rounded corners, undated, tempera on paper / Wim Crouwel, New Alphabet, 'alfabet', c. 1964, tempera on paper

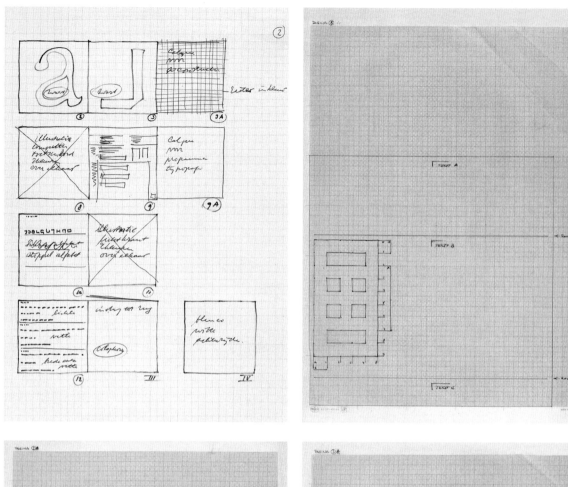

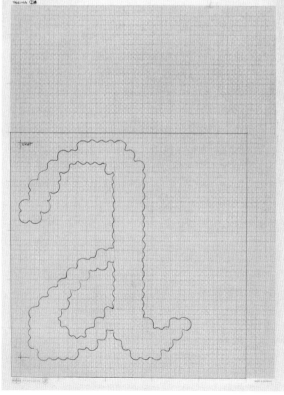

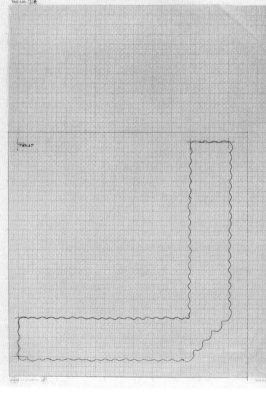

Wim Crouwel, sketch for the 'Quadrat' edition of the New Alphabet, letter A, c. 1966, ink on graph paper (2x)

In 1961 Wim Crouwel posed a fundamental question: 'Of what does modern typography consist? I am currently wrestling with this issue. As my starting point I am using a single basis form, which through optical means can produce bold, light, and italic versions and so forth, according to my needs. With this kind of standardised letter, which makes no distinction between upper and lower case, one achieves above all a much more relaxed page-image. This is of great importance considering the current pace of life and reading. But a great deal more can be done; the letters and the pages can be considered as elements of the definitive form that one wishes to achieve. The text itself will then more closely resemble an illustration.'

This heralded one of the most interesting experiments in type design in the second half of the twentieth century. It was concerned as much with gauging the limits of the recognisability of letters as with the drive towards a mono-alphabet. In October 1965, during the international *Vision '65* congress in Carbondale, Illinois, Crouwel presented the *New Alphabet*. The letters and numbers were constructed from a basic form. According to Crouwel it was unnecessary to use different forms for the capitals, which could simply be indicated by a horizontal line above the individual letters. A line under the letters indicated the doubling of constituent signs: the 'n' thus became an 'm' and a 'v' became a 'w'. All letters are of the same height and width and so can be ranged in an orderly fashion next to and underneath each other. Another characteristic resulting from the uniform spacing is the so-called 'English alignment': the lines do not necessarily need to be filled entirely, but may be may be 'ragged'. Crouwel designed the typeface entirely by hand, without the aid of technology, as if the computer were a mere post-rationalisation, a convenient frame within which to present a typeface at that historical moment. From a perceptual point of view, it is somewhat difficult to read: the alphabet is not very functional, but places the emphasis on the aesthetic aspect of the technological imagery. It is an artistic expression, whereby 'function follows form.'

Wim Crouwel, sketch for the 'Quadrat' edition of the New Alphabet, cover text, c.1966, ink on graph paper

Wim Crouwel, sketch for the 'Quadrat' edition of the New Alphabet, structure of the points, c. 1966, tempera on card

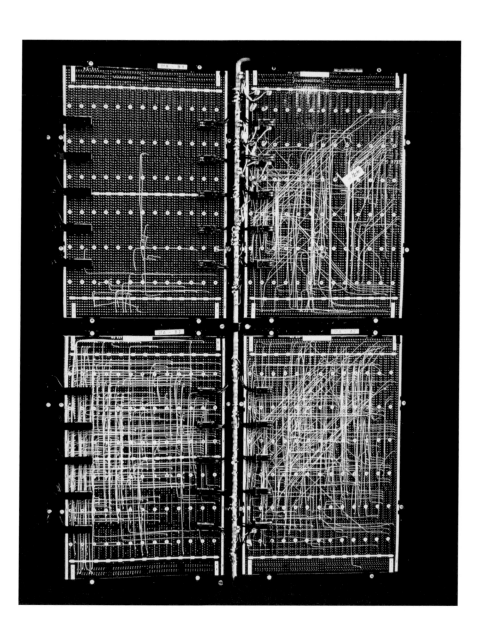

Illustration from the 'Quadrat' edition of the *New Alphabet*

literature
Wim Crouwel, *Kwadratenblad New Alphabet*, Amsterdam 1967
Kees Broos, *Wim Crouwel Alphabets*, Amsterdam 2003

Kho Liang Ie/Artifort/Dynamiet Nobel, prototype for the *modular cupboard system KTS*, 1970, aluminium, plastics, height 220 cm

Modular Cupboard System KTS 1970

Kho Liang Ie (1927-1975)

1

For example
the *Combi
Center* from
1963 and the
*Man-Woman
Container* from
1964. A year
after Kho's
design followed
Colombo's
*Total Furnishing
Unit*. See
I. Favata, *Joe
Colombo and
Italian Design
of the Sixties*,
London 1988.

When he worked on the KTS programme together with Geoffrey Harcourt in 1970, Kho Liang Ie had already created an international furore with his furniture design, exhibition stands and interiors projects. From 1957 he mapped out the artistic direction of Artifort, for whom he produced numerous designs. Under his guidance Artifort was transformed from a sleepy Dutch company producing 'comfortable' furniture, into an internationally trend-setting manufacturer of avant-garde furniture. Through his generosity he made room within the team for other important designers such as Pierre Paulin and Geoffrey Harcourt. Artifort's new range was characterised by modern uphol-stered furniture in bright colours with a perfect feel for topicality.

The concept for the KTS programme came from a commission by Artifort and the German plastics supplier Dynamiet Nobel. The start-ing point was to combine the functions of sitting, sleeping, storage, eating and working each in a single unit. Kho, who designed the units, was inspired by the bamboo basketwork cabin trunks with leather bands, in which people in Indonesia transported all their worldly goods. Harcourt designed the seating elements.

The units, which were conceived in three sizes, should accommodate the entire belongings of a single person. The boxes consisted of aluminium modular elements with polyester sliding doors. Pre-fabrication and standardisation, which was essential to Kho's thinking, originated from the work of designers such as Richard Buckminster Fuller and Joe Colombo. During the 1960s Colombo had already made various attempts to house different living functions within units.[1] The idea of storing the entire contents of a home within moveable units, however, was entirely new, and shows just how visionary Kho's thinking was. This revolutionary idea of modular, standardised components and a rounded design anticipate the large interiors commissions that Kho would later realise, such as those for Phonogram, the Lijnbaan Theatre and, of course, Schiphol Airport.

It is a shame that the KTS system was not put into production. Problems with patents, marketing, financing and plastic's negative image in the light of the oil crisis contributed to this.

literature

Ineke van Ginneke, *Kho Liang Ie, interieurarchitect/industrieel ontwerper*, Rotterdam 1986

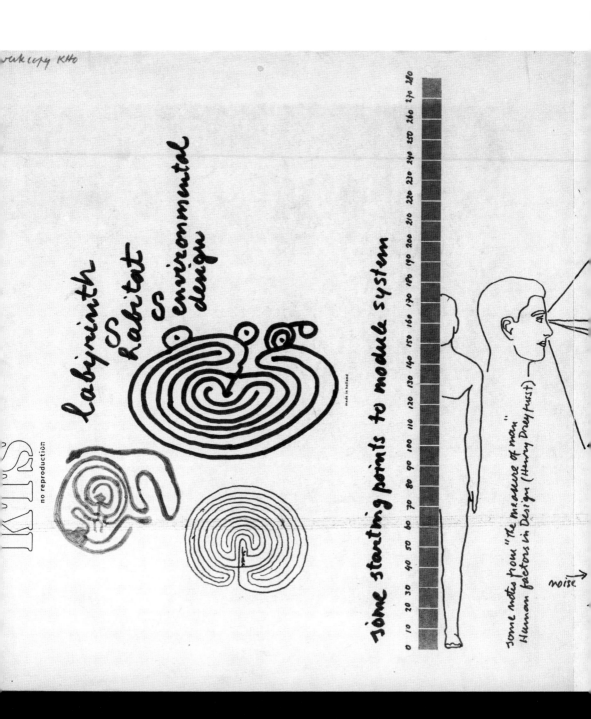

Labyrinth
Rabitat
S
environmental design

made in holland

some starting points to module system

0 10 20 30 40 50 60 70 80 90 100 110 120 130 140 150 160 170 180 190 200 210 220 230 240 250 260 270 280

some notes from "The measure of man"
Human factors in Design (Henry Dreyfuss)

noise

this book Kho Liang Ie presented the dimensional system (based on

160

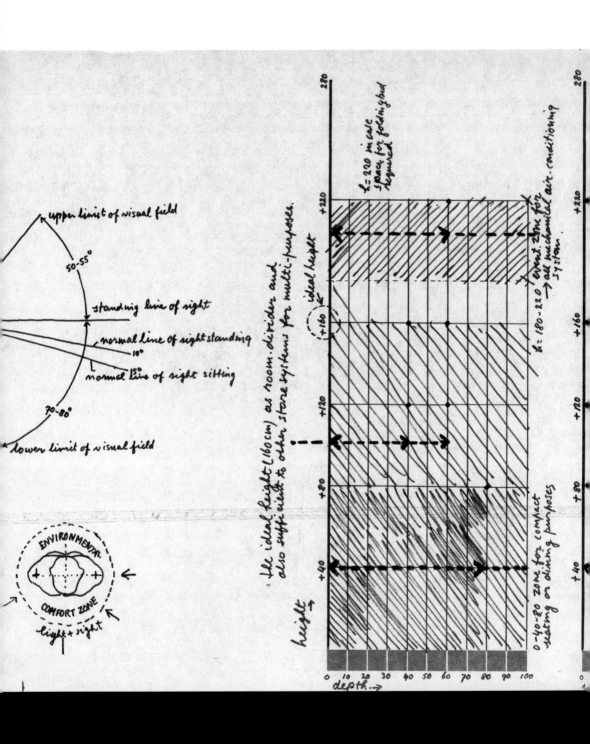

upper limit of visual field

50-55°

standing line of sight

normal line of sight standing

10°

15°

normal line of sight sitting

70-80°

lower limit of visual field

ENVIRONMENTAL

COMFORT ZONE

light + right

" the ideal height (160 cm) as room-divider and also sufficient to other store systems for multi-purposes.

height →

ideal height

+160

height scale: 280, 220, 160, 120, 80, 40

L = 220 in cave space for folding bed required

L = 180-220 exact. zone for → all mechanical air-conditioning system

0-40-80 zone for compact stating or dining purposes

depth →

0 10 20 30 40 50 60 70 80 90 100

280

220

160

120

80

40

0

the ideas of Henry Dreyfuss), the module, the storage function, the

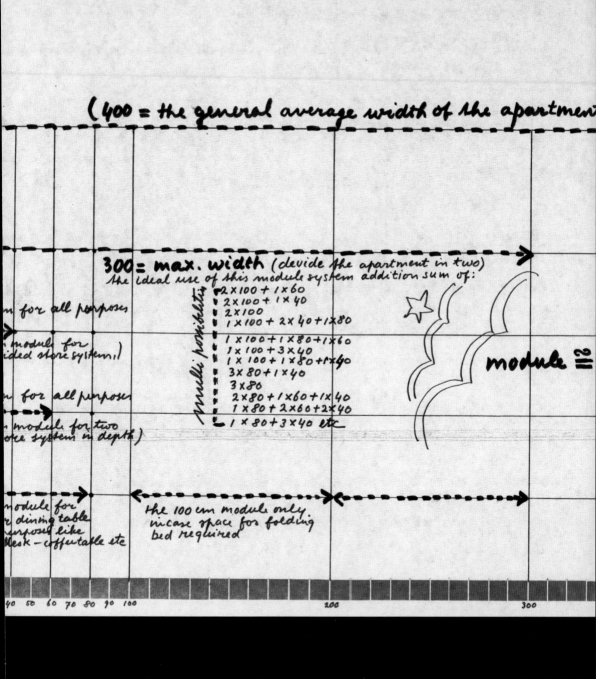

(400 = the general average width of the apartment

300 = **max. width** (devide the apartment in two)
the ideal use of this module system addition sum of:

multi possibilities

2×100 + 1×60
2×100 + 1×40
2×100
1×100 + 2×40 + 1×80

1×100 + 1×80 + 1×60
1×100 + 3×40
1×100 + 1×80 + 1×40
3×80 + 1×40
3×80
2×80 + 1×60 + 1×40
1×80 + 2×60 + 2×40
1×80 + 3×40 etc

module 112

n for all purposes

module for
ided store system.)

n for all purposes

module for two
ore system in depth)

module for
r dining table
urposes like
lesk - coffeetable etc

the 100 cm module only.
incase space for folding
bed required

40 50 60 70 80 90 100   200   300

onstruction and the sleeping, sitting and eating/working functions.

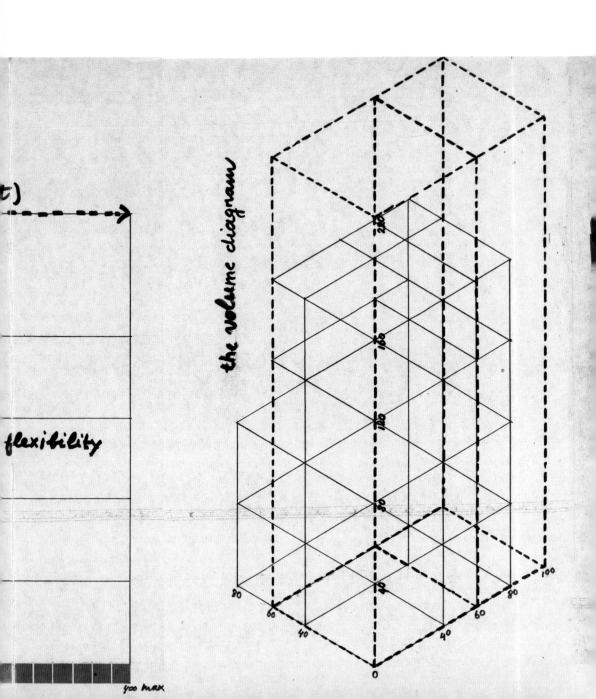

t)

flexibility

the volume diagram

400 max

80
60
40
40
60
80
100
0
40
80
120
160
200

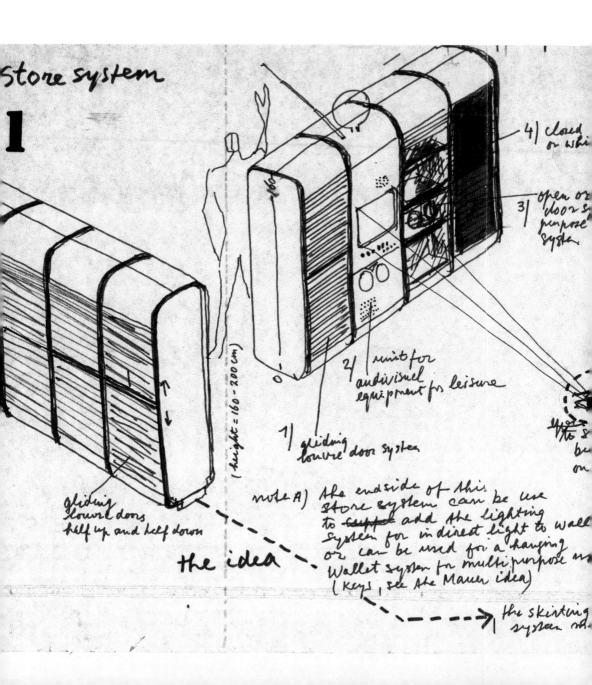

store system

1

4) closed
or whi

3) open or
door s
purpose
system

2) units for
audivisual
equipment for leisure

1) gliding
louvre door system

(height = 160 - 200 cm)

gliding
louvre doors
half up and half down

note A) the endside of this
store system can be use
to ~~suppl~~ add the lighting
system for indirect light to wall
or can be used for a hanging
wallet system for multipurpose us
(keys, see the Mauer idea)

the idea

the skirting
system sor.

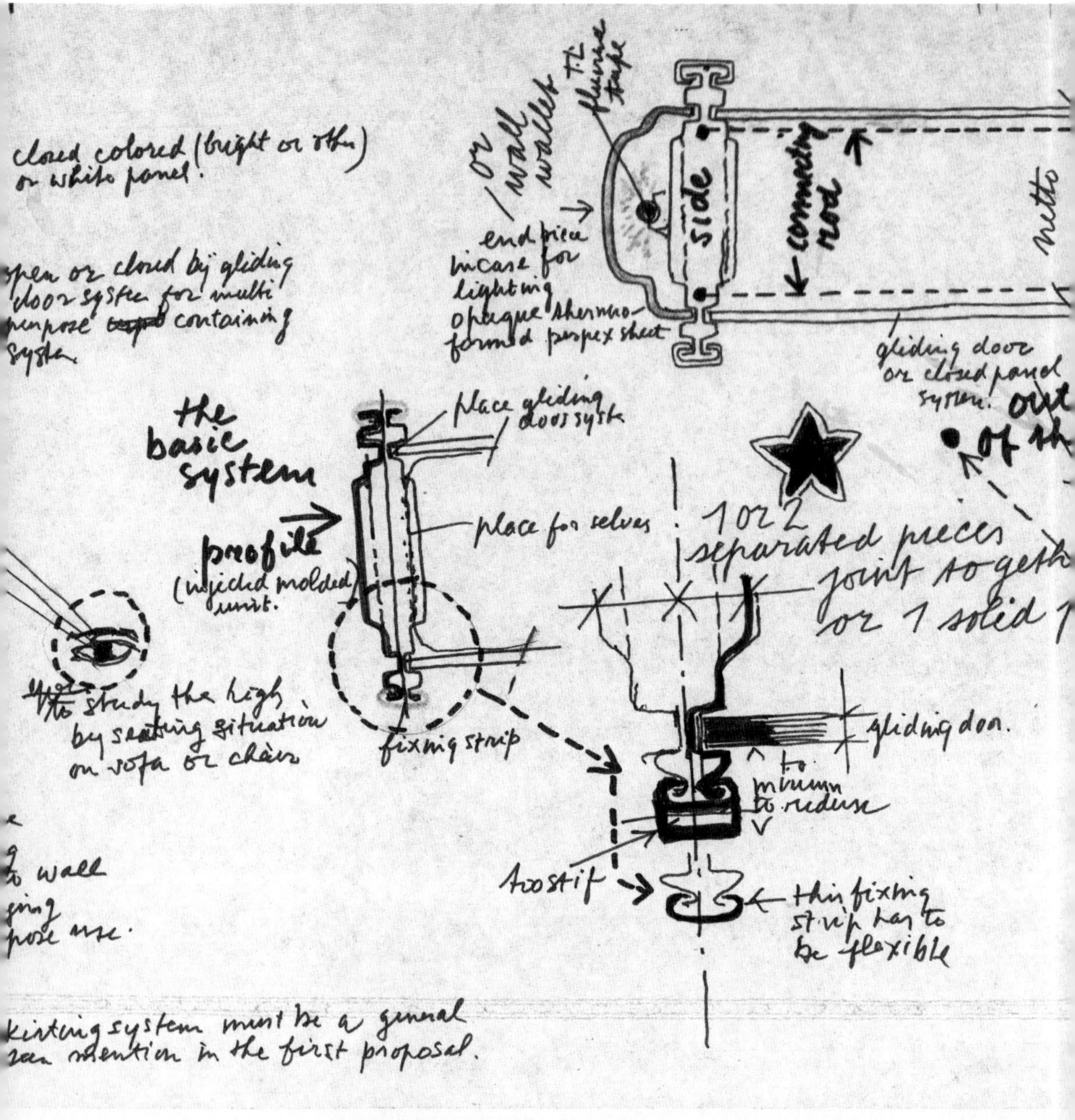

closed colored (bright or other)
or white panel.

open or closed by gliding
door system for multi
purpose ~~box~~ containing
system

the
basic
system

profile
(injected molded
unit.

to study the high.
by seating situation
on sofa or chair

fixing strip

to wall
ping
pose use.

fixing system must be a general
~~~ intention in the first proposal.

or
wall
wallet

TL
fluorine
tupe

end piece
incase for
lighting
opaque thermo-
formed perspex sheet

side

connecting
rod

netto

gliding door
or closed panel
system. out
of th

place gliding
door system

place for selves

1 or 2
separated pieces
joint togeth
or 1 solid 1

gliding door

to
minimum
to reduce

too stiff

thin fixing
strip has to
be flexible

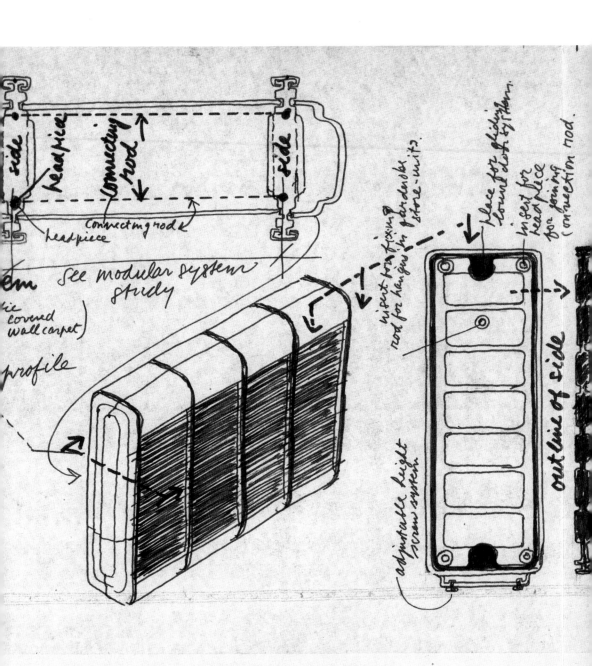

side

headpiece

connecting rod

Connecting rod

headpiece

See modular system study

(covered wall carpet)

profile

adjustable height screw system

insert for fixing rod for hanger in wardrobe store-units

place for sliding round cloth system

insert for headpiece for joining (connection rod)

outline of side

166

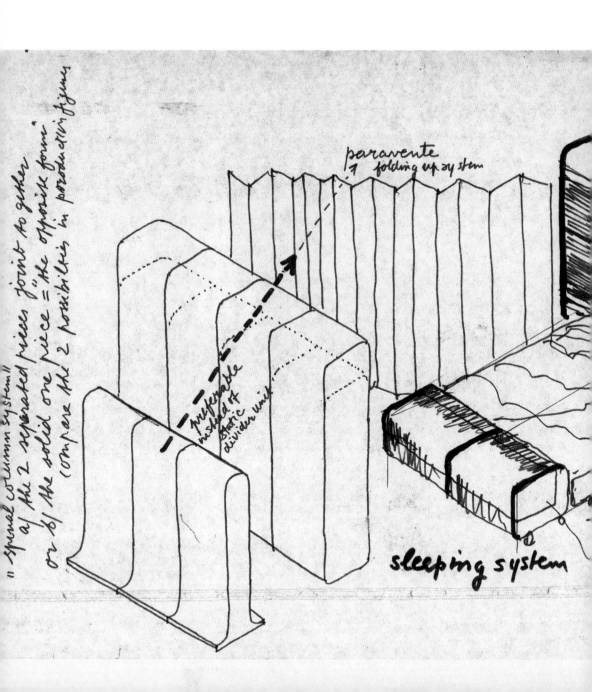

paravente
↑ folding up system

" spinal column system!!
a/ the 2 separated pieces joint together
or b/ the solid one piece = "the opposite form"
compare the 2 possibilities in productiv figures

preferable instead of static divider unit

sleeping system

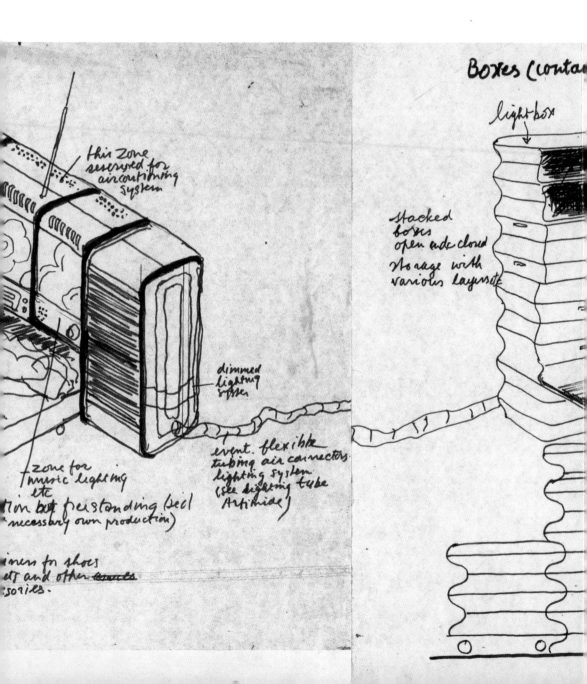

this Zone
reserved for
air conditioning
system

Boxes (contai

light box

stacked
boxes
open ends closed
storage with
various layers etc

dimmed
lighting
system

event. flexible
tubing air connectors
lighting system
(see lighting tube
Artimide)

zone for
music lighting
etc
tion but freestanding (secl
necessary own production)

iners for shoes
ets and other ~~tools~~
ssories.

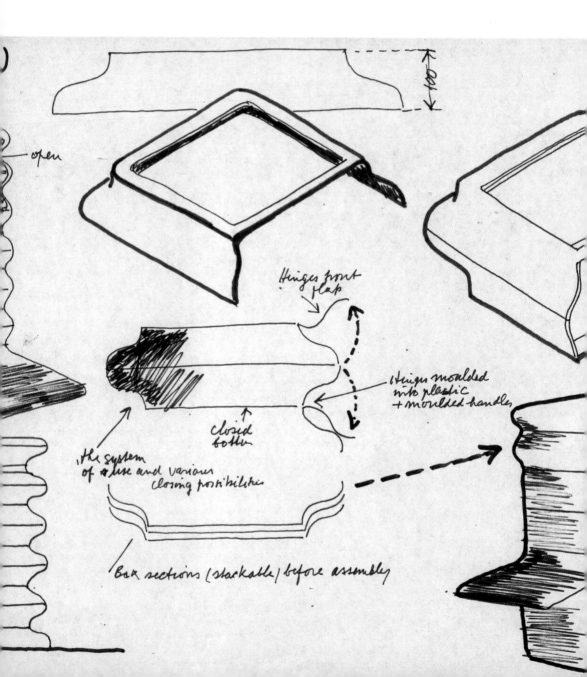

open

Hinges front flap

Hinges moulded into plastic + moulded handles.

closed bottom

the system of *use and various closing possibilities

Box sections (stackable) before assembly

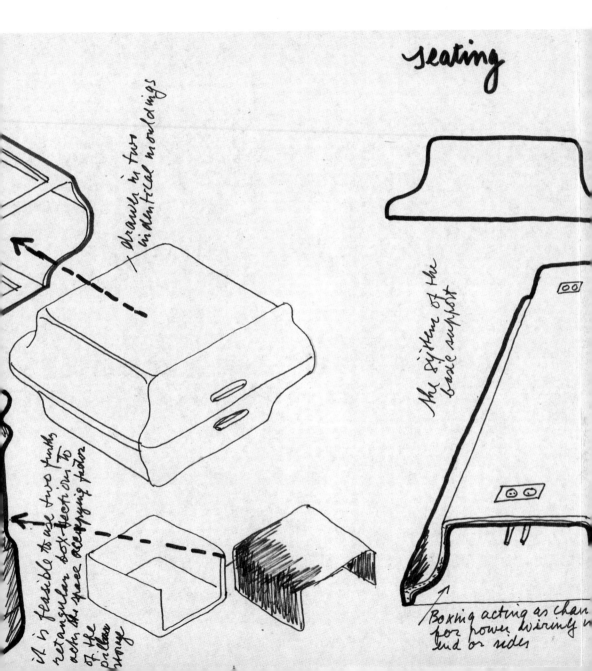

seating

drawer in two identical mouldings

the system of the base support

it is feasible to use two truth rectangular box-section to adn the space occupying them of the pillar wing

Boxing acting as chan for power wiring in end or sides

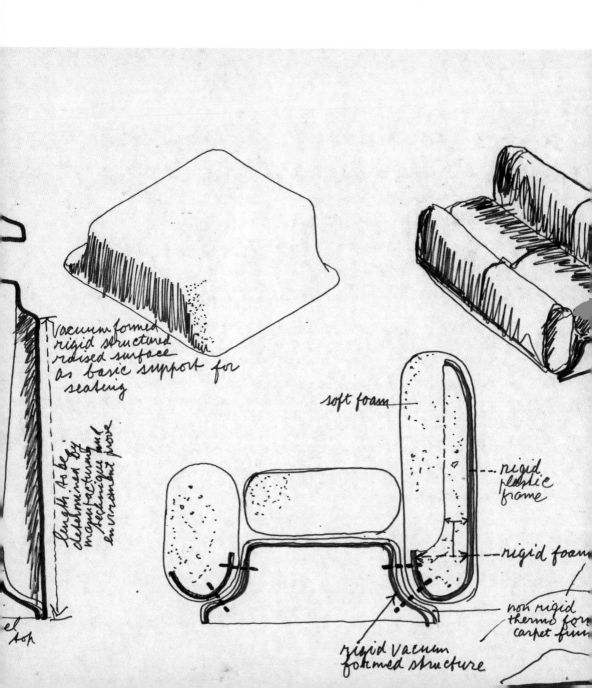

Vacuum formed
rigid structured
raised surface
as basic support for
seating

Length to be
determined by
manufacturing
technique and
environment above

soft foam

rigid
plastic
frame

rigid foam

non rigid
thermo for
carpet finish

rigid vacuum
formed structure

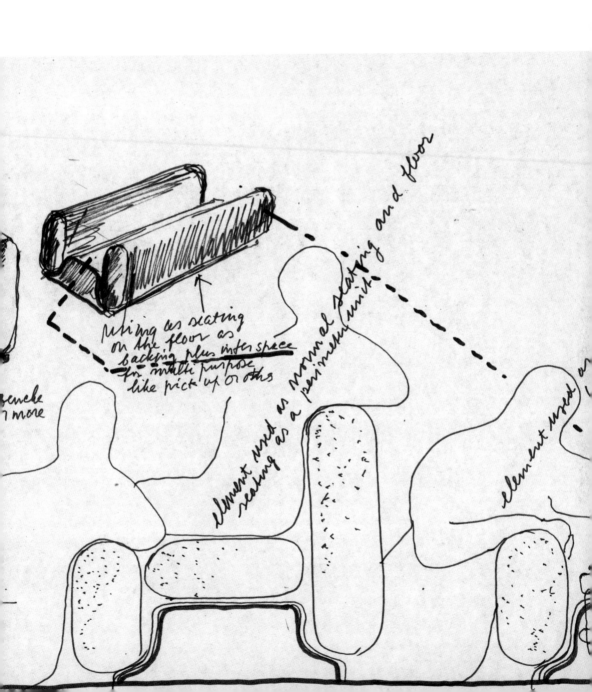

using as seating
on the floor as
backing plus interspace
for multi purpose
like pick up or others

element used as normal seating and floor

seating as a perimeter unit

bench
more

element used a

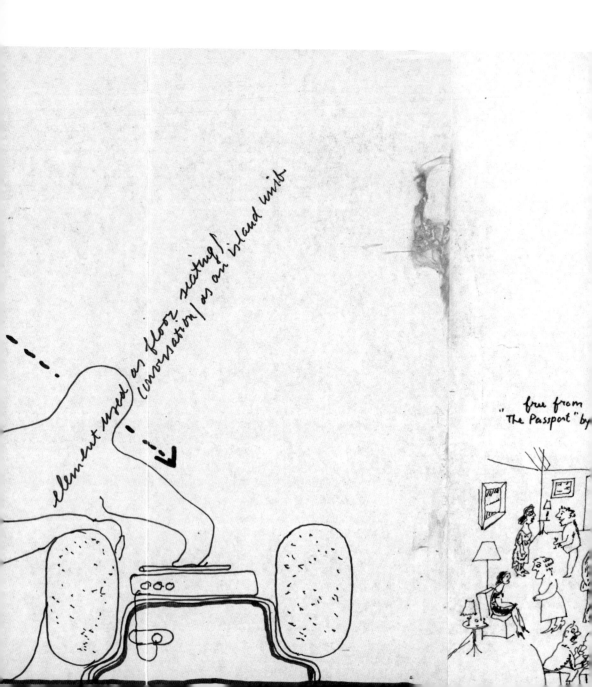

element used as floor seating /
(conversation) as an island unit
drawn up no as an island unit

free from
"The Passport" by

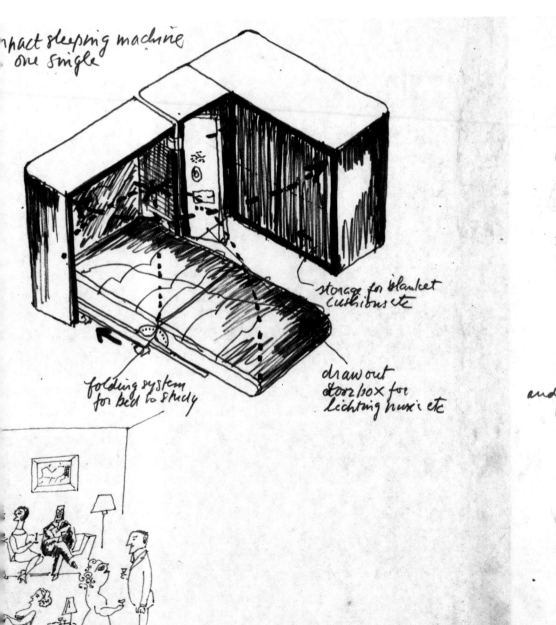

compact sleeping machine
one single

storage for blanket
cushions etc

folding system
for bed to study

draw out
door/box for
lighting music etc

to
glas
clin
sn

oth
Kee
and pre
food

dining or working

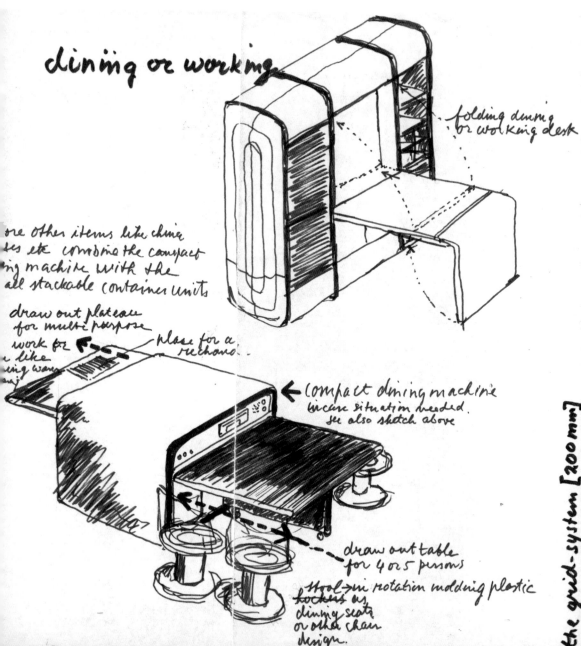

folding dining
or working desk

...ore other items like china
...ses etc. combine the compact
...ing machine with the
...all stackable container units

draw out plateau
for multi-purpose
work for
...e like
...ing ware
...

place for a
recharge

← compact dining machine
incase situation needed.
see also sketch above

draw out table
for 4 or 5 persons

stool → in rotation molding plastic
lockers as
dining seats
or other chair
design.

the grid-system [200 mm]

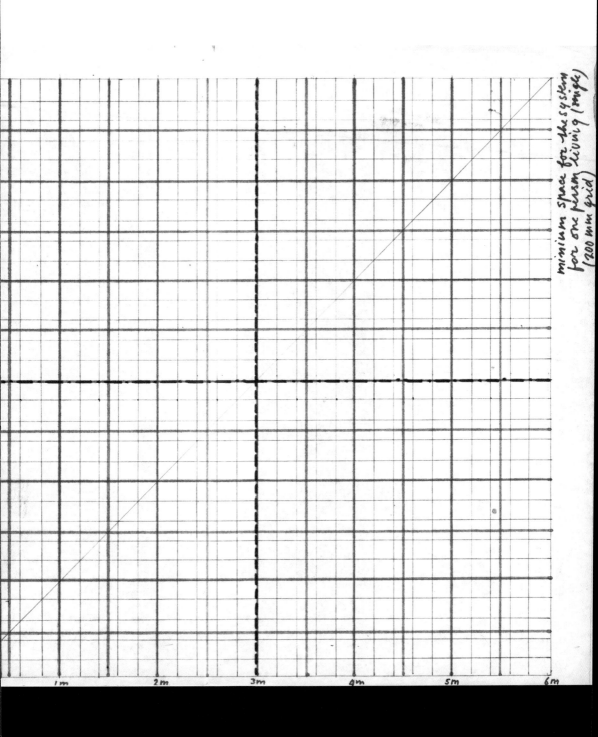

minimum space for the system for one person living (single) (200 mm grid)

1 m   2 m   3 m   4 m   5 m   6 m

e German company KTS (Kunsttechnologische Studiën Gesellschaft) had undertaken studies of future forms of living and their consequences
new furniture. From his, unfortunately unrealised, design for the KTS programme it appears that Kho thought in systems and also experimented
the field of plastics applications. In addition the design is of consequence because it led to later plastic box systems that were realised.
n Ginneke 1986, p. 140, note 58

Bicchiere Imbevibile 1970

Alessandro Mendini (1931)

Alessandro Mendini was born in Milan in 1931. Until 1970 he worked in the architectural studio of Nizzoli Associati. Thereafter he became the editor-in-chief of Casabella and became deeply involved with the Architettura Radicale. He took part in Global Tools and was a co-founder of Studio Alchimia, within which he developed the concept of Banal Design. The basis of this concept was that in a society completely dominated by mass culture there was little left for a designer to do than to cynically manipulate the mass culture. Since 1977 Mendini has advised the firm Alessi, for whom he has coordinated many much-discussed projects such as the Tea & Coffe Piazza (1983) and the Casa della Felicità, and also shops, fair stands and even a museum. Mendini also designs shop interiors for Swatch and has recently built metro stations in Naples, on which he worked closely with visual artists. He also publishes a videozine.

Architettura Radicale
Anti-design originated in England
(Archigram, 1961) and Austria,
where designers such as Hans Hollein
and Pichler experimented with ideas
from the tradition of German
Expressionism. A key figure in Italy
was Ettore Sottsass Jr., who published
in Casabella – the mouthpiece of the
Italian counter-movement, and
assembled many young designers
around him. After 1975 the
conceptually tinted anti-design was
absorbed within the capitalist system.
Studio Alchimia (1976) became its
client, producer, salesman and
exhibitor. Memphis (1981-1987),
which very self-consciously launched
a collection each year, was also a
channel for transforming its concepts
into saleable products.

*Glass in de form of a pistol, seventeenth century,
Belgium, length 38 cm*

It speaks for itself that drinking from
this pistol during drinking games
must have made a bizarre impression
upon onlookers.

The conical Bicchiere Imbevibile, the
Undrinkable Glass , by Alessandro
Mendini is made not of glass, but of
bronze.[1] Furthermore, it is so flat and
heavy that it is almost impossible to pick
it up, let alone to drink from it. Why
does a designer create an unusable
object? Mendini made it at the end of the
1960s when, frustrated with the design
practice current at the time, he gave up
his position at Nizzoli Associati. The
dangers of the consumer society –
environmental damage and over-
consumption – were slowly becoming
apparent. Why would one want to design
something new when so many good
things already existed? Above all, many
designers were concerned that they were
merely designing status symbols for the
ruling class rather than utilitarian objects
for the masses. Slowly a politicised
design movement developed in Italy, the
Architettura Radicale, which mounted a
critique of capitalism. In their spare time
the members organised carnivalesque
protest happenings.[2]

Within this atmosphere the Bicchiere
Imbevibile was born as part of the series
'Oggetti ad uso spirituali' (Objects for
spiritual use), which also included a bed
with the bedstead in the form of Mount
Calvary and a chair with an enormous
crucifix in its back. It was as if Mendini
asked himself: who could have a problem
with falling asleep under Mount Calvary?
In addition to setting himself against
the well-to-do Catholic milieu of his
hometown Milan[3], Mendini was also
commenting on the ideology of 'form
follows function'. This dominant methodology viewed design exclusively from a

1
In 1984
Museum
Boijmans V
Beuningen
acquired t
wooden
model. The
bronze ori
belongs to
Mendini.
2
For more
informatio
anti-desigr
see: Exh. c
*Italy: the N
Domestic
Landscape*
New York
(MOMA) 19
3
Frans Haks
*Alessandro
Mendini
schetsboek*
Groningen
1988, p. 6

4
Alessandro
Mendini,
Rosamaria
Rinaldi (ed.),
*Progetto
Infelice*, Milan
1983, p. 10
5
Exh. cat.,
*Entworfene
Malerei,
gemalte
Entwürfe*,
Ahlen (Kunst-
museum)
1997, p. 7

functional perspective and allowed little room for the emotional needs of the user. It was for this reason that Mendini intentionally made his glass unusable. The design principle of the Bicchiere Imbevibile stems from the Surrealists. It refers to Man Ray's 'Cadeau Audace' from 1921 – a flatiron with tacks attached to its base – or to Meret Oppenheim's 'Object' from 1936 – a fur covered cup, saucer and spoon, which according to Mendini were the most celebrated objects in the history of avant-garde design, and without which the 'radical' design of the 1960s would have been far less so.[4] The originality of Mendini's approach was to position himself as a visual artist, using visual means such as association, ambiguity and irony.

Man Ray, *Cadeau Audace*, 1921/1974 edition 36/300, iron, height 16.5 cm

ly work has its deepest source in my nature as a painter. herefore I speak of painted design and designed painting. ..] In my case design concepts always have their origins painterly ideas.[5]

He considered planning and efficiency,
tenets central to functionalism, as increasingly less
appropriate to construct the world.

'I increasingly believe that it is more important to paint than to plan. […] Painting is a cycle: everything that must happen has already happened and the individual's reflection is free to move in every direction, through all cultures and places, as long as it acts on the basis of sincerity.'[6]

With his Proust Armchair of 1978 Mendini came to a radical conclusion. He painted a pseudo-eighteenth-century easy chair with pointilliste brushmarks in the manner of Paul Signac. He re-used existing images from art and design history and put the aura of painting into perspective by turning it into the decoration for a chair – a painting for sitting on. He continued to develop this principle of redesign, above all within Studio Alchimia.

Alessandro Mendini, *Proust Armchair*, 1978

Alessandro Mendini/Alessi, *100% Make Up*, 1992

Aliessandro Mendini, *Groninger Museum*, 1987-1994

Alessandro Mendini/Alessi, *100% Make Up*, 1992

Mendini was active for many years as editor-in-chief, firstly at Casabella (1970-1976), then at Modo, which he set up himself (1977-1979) and from 1979 at Domus. Frans Haks described him as someone who designs in the way that one lays out a publication: 'I view the Groninger Museum very much as an issue of a magazine, full of stirring articles written by different authors. Mendini was one of the first to invite different designers and architects to work on a single project. Architects, designers and painters worked together on his Mobile Infinito from 1981, designing its various parts, and the *Tea & Coffee Piazza* and *100% Make Up* for Alessi were set up following the same principle.'

6
Ibid., p.140
7
Conversation
with Frans Haks,
Amsterdam,
20 January 2003

When designing something Mendini dives into the product's cultural history and, like an alchemist, mixes everything that he considers usable. Frans Haks, who selected Mendini to design the new Groninger Museum, puts it as follows:

Mendini couldn't give a damn about the need to be original. I learned from him to put the twentieth century's fixation with originality into perspective. Throughout the whole of history artists and architects have referred to the past and to each other, but art theoreticians and critics won't allow that. Mendini always plants a bomb under people's notions of what is and is not allowed, and anyone who does that has any unconditional support.[7]

information
www.mendini.it

Michele de Lucchi/Girmi/Rabbolini, *prototype vacuum cleaner*, 1979, painted wood, plastics, length 48 cm (detail)

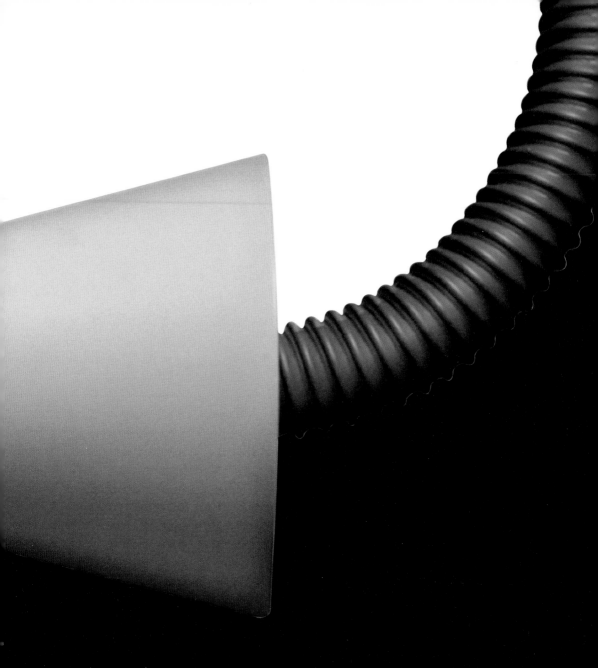

Prototypes 1979

Michele de Lucchi (1951)

At the Milan Triennale in 1979 the Italian designer Michele de Lucchi presented eleven prototypes for, amongst other things, a coffee grinder, a vacuum cleaner, a toaster, an iron and a hairdryer, all commissioned by the Italian company Girmi. Although they were non-functioning and made of wood, they appeared deceptively real, even down to the power cables. With these toy-like objects, De Lucchi made it clear that while domestic appliances may appear anonymous, they are nonetheless subject to fashionable trends. De Lucchi defined the matt-black aesthetic of the German and Japanese electronic products that flooded the market at the end of the 1970s, and which had little to do with most consumers' everyday environments, as one-dimensional, technological and almost military: 'From the television to the iron, from the stereo installation to the kettle, nowadays everything is technologic-ally designed. The more vents, knobs, metres, indicators and connections there are on an appliance, the more beautiful people find it. So that a beautiful woman is forced to blow-dry her hair with an appliance that looks more like a laser pistol than a hairdryer.'[1]

With their pastel pink shades and familiar forms, his prototypes reminded one of the 1950s, a period that De Lucchi had studied thoroughly two years earlier when he worked on a large exhibition of 1950s Italian design. However, it was not so much the fifties, but more so popular culture in general that gave this series its identity. He consciously referred to the world of comic strips, science fiction and the punk movement, but in a very considered manner. De Lucchi: 'My reference points are not refined culture, but Disneyland and America. My culture is made of immediate sensations.' De Lucchi is a serious industrial designer and the creator of, amongst other things, the Tolomeo Lamp for Artemide, which has become a classic of the 1990s. Indeed, in retrospect the prototypes appear less exuberant than one may have initially thought. They are not decorated; are dominated by the primary colours yellow and blue – supplemented with green and pink – and the forms are predominantly geometric.

In the *International Design Yearbook* that he compiled in 2001, De Lucchi wrote: 'My profession is not to be a designer or an architect – it is to make a bridge between industry and humanity' [2]

According to him the relationship between people and their implements should not be aggressive, but rather friendly, intimate, playful, passive and sensual. He wants appliances to have a skin, an erotic body that is not subordinated to the mechanical, but is rather an active stimulant for the imagination.[3] Although his prototypes have their roots in popular culture, they are not the ironic exercises in kitsch produced by Alessandro Mendini. [4] De Lucchi remains faithful to the archetypes, the generic models of domestic appliances, to which he applies humour and sensuality.

Two years after the exhibition of the domestic appliances *Domus* published De Lucchi's sketches for stereo equipment, radios and televisions. They were a progression of the domestic appliances, but he now also experimented with black and white punk-like decoration. De Lucchi: 'We live in an age of consumerism. Our means of communication is dictated by mass production. (...) The matt-black finish is the image of the 1970s. Now we are open to the possibilities of decoration. Decoration is the design challenge of the 1980s.'[5]

Although De Lucchi viewed his domestic appliances as a quasi-scientific experiment, he would have liked to have seen them in production. But they were not released on the market and neither was the stereo equipment. It was therefore more than simply an exercise in style. A few years later he described these experiments as too one-sided, when he wrote: 'The market does not want revolutions, but rather evolutions of itself.'[6]

1
C. Donà, 'Un Designer Gentile', *Zoom attualita*, z.j., pp. 10-11

2
International Design Yearbook, London, 2001, p. 6

3
F. Alinovi, 'Hi-fi secondo M. de Lucchi', *Domus* 617 (1981), pp. 38-40

4
P. Sparke 'De Lucchi designs: toys for adults', *Industrial Design*, Nov/Dec. (1981) pp. 15 and 57

5
F. Alinovi, 'Hi-fi secondo M. de Lucchi', *Domus* 617 (1981), pp. 38-40

6
M. Ghermandi, 'Michele de Lucchi', *Juliet Art Magazine* 12 (1983)

information
www.produzioneprivata.it

Michele de Lucchi/Girmi/Rabbolini, *prototype hairdryer*, 1979, painted wood, height 21 cm

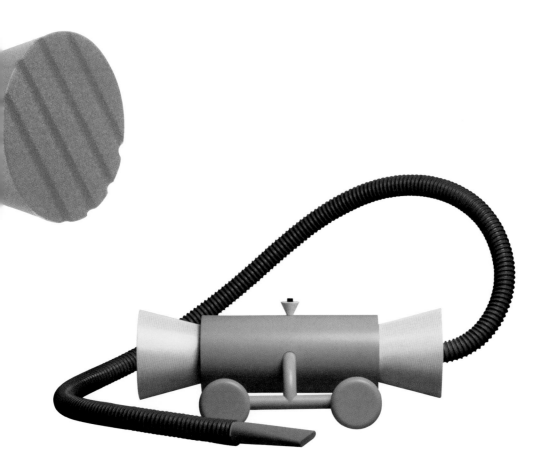

Michele de Lucchi/Girmi/Rabbolini, *prototype vacuum cleaner*, 1979, painted wood, plastics, length 48 cm

Memphis

The domestic appliances appealed to many people's taste, according to De Lucchi, but not to that of designers. This was precisely the aim. Together with other designers including his friend, mentor and Memphis founder Ettore Sottsass, De Lucchi formed a small international group of rebels that shook up the design world in the early 1980s. The Memphis designers campaigned against the 'form follows function' ideology, which – in their eyes – had a stranglehold on the profession and which left barely any room for a more playful design method. The Memphis designers found their inspiration in mass culture. In a similar way to the fashion industry, for seven years Memphis presented annual collections in which the designers ironically inverted the functionalist norms.

Michele de Lucchi

De Lucchi was born in Ferrara in 1951
and studied architecture in Florence.
After his studies he moved to Milan,
where he joined the groups Cavart and
Alchimia. In 1981 he was one of the
co-founders of Memphis and established
himself as a free-lance designer. His
practice grew quickly and he now heads
a large company with offices in Milan
and Rome. His clients include Artemide,
Kartell, Poltrona Frau and Olivetti, of
which he has been Director of Design
since 1992. He has designed offices
and office systems for Deutsche Bank,
Deutsche Bundesbahn, Poste Italiane
and Telecom Italia. He has worked for
Vitra, Philips, Compaq, Siemens, and
Kembo and has designed architectural
projects in Italy, Germany and Japan.
He is the recipient of numerous
international prizes and has taught at
the University of Venice since 2001.

Produzione Privata

De Lucchi has always designed products in small series. In 1990 he established Produzione Privata, a business with a cultural and ideological character in the spirit of the Wiener Werkstätte. In the designs for Produzione Privata he follows his intuition and his own ideas, independent of the demands of industrial marketing. The form of his products, which he produces in batches and distributes himself, is dictated not by the market but by reflections on material culture. He works closely with craftspeople, whose knowledge and skills are threatened with extinction. He combines their handiwork with the newest techniques. In opposition to the exuberance of Memphis' products, those of Produzione Privata consist mainly of discreet and simple household objects and lighting.

Roulandt
1981-1983

Max 1986

Aart Roelandt
(1954)

Max is a prototype, with which
andt anticipated future
nologies. The transmission
ld occur via cords, a fine chain
dynamo with an electric motor.
electrical energy would be
red in a special, conductive
tic. Roelandt also wanted to
rporate a Global Positioning
tem (GPS) so that you couldn't
lost, as well as a 'personal coach'
would register your sporting
omplishments. 'I am fascinated
echnology. I have not completely
ed all the technical aspects that
posed in this prototype but in
ciple they are realistic. I call
elf a practical idealist and seek
ant solutions to problems that
int out.

In 1981 Roelandt graduated with honours with a recumbent bicycle, for which he later received the incentive prize from the City of Amsterdam. During his studies at the Academy for Industrial Design in Eindhoven he performed an internship at Gazelle. He already had ideas for a recumbent bicycle, but was not allowed to design: he first had to familiarise himself intimately with the fabrication process. For his graduation examination Roelandt built two models, one with the academy's workshop assistant and the other with a bicycle maker from Velthoven. This latter model was chromed and had closed wheels – a rarity at the time – in order to minimise drag. Following his graduation Roelandt joined forces with an engineering firm to ready the bicycle for production. They developed four prototypes to determine the ergonomically correct position. The handlebars were moved to below the seat, making steering easier. Two years and approximately five-hundred test-rides later the design was complete and the team had the bicycle produced in large quantities. It was named the Roulandt, a wordplay on the French word *rouler* – to roll – and the designer's surname. However, both parties were unable to agree on the division of the royalties and the partnership came to an end. Nonetheless, Roelandt reckons that between two and seven thousand examples were produced and sold from America to Australia, where the packaging promised: 'To ride it is to love it.'

The brakes were activated by hand-grips under the handlebars. Braking by peddling backwards would also have been possible, but was less suitable due to the length of the transmission chain. Although the bike appears to be quite long, it is in fact a

Scientific research later proved that the recumbent position causes exactly the same physical stress as the traditional riding position.

A racing bike causes pain in the back, the seat, the wrists and the stomach, which is squeezed up. Moreover visibility is limited. I asked myself how I would prefer to cycle, and discovered that you could see more if you leaned back, as in an armchair. You sit comfortably and look straight ahead rather than at the wheels; your sightline runs parallel with the horizon.

mere fifteen centimetres longer than a conventional bicycle. It can be adjusted to a maximum of 190 centimetres, making it unsuited to very tall people. The Roulandt weighs only twelve kilograms and is easily carried up stairs.

The principle of the recumbent bicycle is not new. Aart Roelandt: 'It seems that there were already recumbent bicycles in 1898. But as far as I know they were never put into production. The Roulandt was the first to be produced serially, and since it appeared on the market at least ten workshops have begun to develop and produce their own models. Five of these were based on my design.'

The Roulandt was acquired by Museum Boijmans Van Beuningen, which invited him in 1986 to design a 'bicycle for the future' to be shown in the exhibition *Sport and Design*. This commission led to the streamlined, cherry-red Max, Roelandt's second recumbent bicycle. It is made entirely of synthetic materials: kevlar fused with carbon fibre and glassfibre, a combination that makes the bike light and strong. In order to be able to ride it, the underside of the bike's wheel housing would have to be raised slightly. Roelandt: 'I wanted to design a fully integrated model. The rear wheel, the crossbar and the pedals form a single whole, the front wheel moves independently. The saddle would be vacuum-formed, tailored to the rider who would attach it to the frame himself or herself. The pedals are incorporated into the cyclist's shoes and click directly onto the frame. The handlebars would consist of revolving handgrips that would send electronic signals to the front wheel, following the "fly by wire" principle as is used in the Airbus and fighter-planes.'

Olivetti ETP 55
1985-1987

Olivetti/Mario Bellini
(1935)

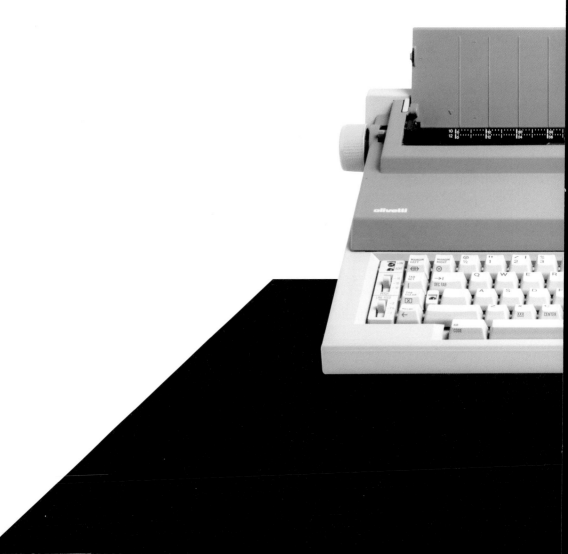

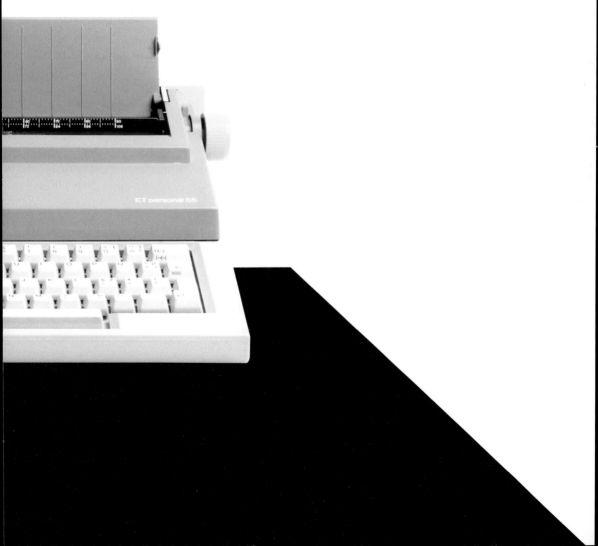

Mario Bellini/Olivetti, ETP 55 portable typewriter, 1987, plastics, metal

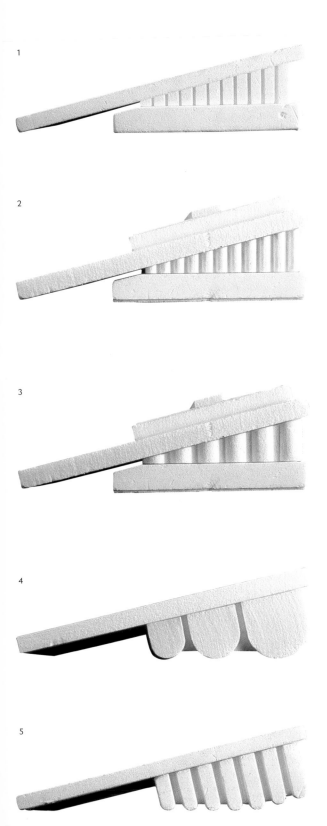

1

2

3

4

5

Olivetti is a company with a huge name in the field of design. Since its establishment in 1908 in Ivrea, a hundred kilometres to the west of Milan, more than sixty leading designers and architects from various countries have designed products and buildings for the company, including Egon Eiermann, Le Corbusier, Vico Magistretti, Richard Meier, George Nelson, Marcello Nizzoli, Ettore Sottsass and Van den Broek and Bakema. Adriano Olivetti, the son of the company's founder, once said of the importance of design within the company, 'Design is the visible, perceptible expression of quality in industrial activity; quality not only in economic terms, but in terms of cultural values.'[1] This conviction comes across not only in Olivetti's products, but also in its graphic design, its architecture and interior design. Commissions have always been granted to designers and architects who have already proved themselves and who subscribe to Olivetti's philosophy.

At Olivetti design does not take place within an isolated department, but is an interactive process between all divisions of the company: the management, the marketing department, the designers, the technicians and the people with eventual responsibility for the production. Its success is based on a sound infrastructure for the sharing of knowledge and experience, cooperative relationships and direct contacts with the international design world. Informal processes always form the driving force behind the development of new products. The process from the initial idea for a product through to its introduction in the market is seldom documented. However, there is some information available

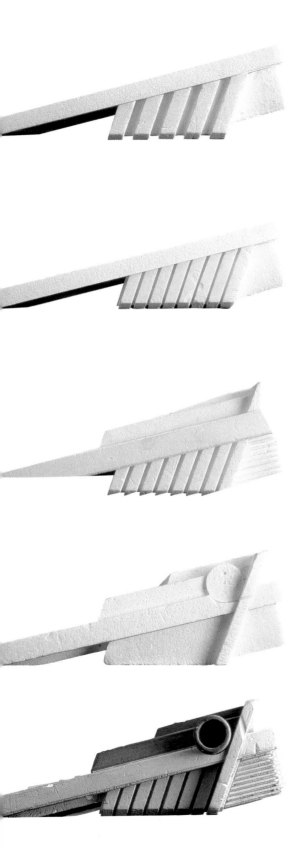

about the development of the ETP 55 portable typewriter that gives an insight into the design process of this Italian manufacturer.

In 1985 Olivetti decided that it was time to replace the Praxis 20 typewriter, which had been launched three years earlier. During this period the market for typewriters had slumped substantially and there was cut-throat competition from other important manufacturers such as Brother, Canon, Nagashima, Olympia and Sharp, which often had far lower production costs because they were based in the Far East. In order to continue to distinguish itself within the typewriter market, two factors were of great importance for Olivetti: quality and design. In August 1985 the development of the ETP55 was officially set in motion.

The marketing department researched the commercial criteria and Mario Bellini, who had designed computers, calculators, typewriters and photocopiers for the company since 1963, was given the task of developing these requirements into a commercially successful product. Allesandro Chiarato played an important part in the process. He advised Bellini on practical capabilities and problems, supervised the technicians from the various departments and was responsible for making the various study models.

The most important requirements of the new product were that it should be cheaper, lighter and smaller, with a contemporary appearance and the most advanced technology. To keep costs as low as possible a technical concept was developed requiring a reduction by fifty per cent of the mechanical components and the re-use of

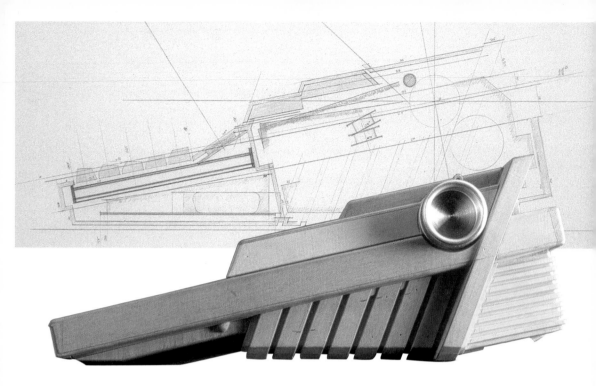

existing components. In addition it was decided to manufacture the product at Olivetti in Singapore. Because durability was of the utmost importance, a metal frame was chosen. The existing Margherita printing system was re-used because the Olivetti experts were of the opinion that it offered the very best printing quality. The exterior appearance of the new typewriter was based on the wedge form that had been introduced by Bellini in 1978, and which had established the image of all subsequent Olivetti typewriters. This form responded excellently to the ergonomic requirements of the consumer market. In addition the new electronic keyboard developed by Olivetti designers King and Miranda fitted perfectly within such a housing.

Bellini made the housing appear smaller by dividing it into separate elements. The volumes of the undercarriage, which house the electronics and the transformer, each have a different pattern of grooves. The individual elements are formally separated from each other by an X-shaped structure, which gives the machine an architectonic quality. As a result, the composition appears not only to be relatively small, light and dynamic, but also fragmented.

A special team within the company, under the leadership of Clino Castelli, had just put the finishing touches to a new colour palette, which was to form Olivetti's future identity. On the basis of the available options Bellini decided to use not only the basis colour – grey – but also blue and yellow; a remarkable step in a period in which most electronic devices were black, grey or white. The result is an attractive and

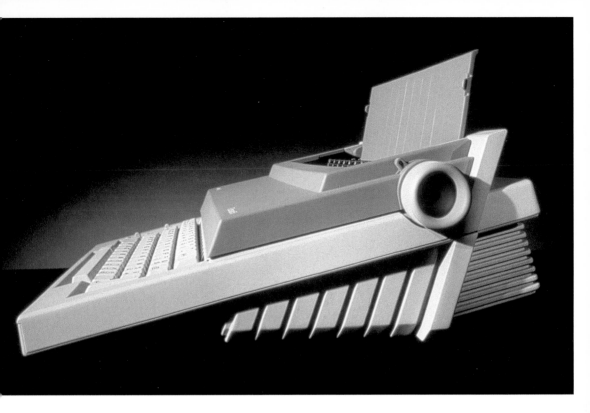

playful product that invites the consumer to use it. In this respect the machine displays a remarkable likeness to the prototypes for domestic appliances that Michele de Lucchi designed a few years earlier for the firm Girmi.

Although explicit references to everyday life are far less frequent in Bellini's designs than in those of De Lucchi and other members of the Memphis group, symbolism nonetheless plays an important role in his work. He himself has described his collection of designs for Olivetti as a herd of strange animals, which can stimulate the user's fantasies and which awaken the desire to tame them as pets. After its presentation at Bellini's solo exhibition at the Museum of Modern Art in New York in 1987, the machine could be bought and domesticated by consumers from 1988.

1
Sibylle Kicherer, *Olivetti, A Study of the Corporate Management of Design*, London 1990, foreword

literature
Renzo Zorzi (ed.), *Design Process, Olivetti 1908-1983*, Ivrea 1983
Cara McCarty, *Mario Bellini, Designer*, New York 1987
Sibylle Kicherer, *Olivetti, A Study of the Corporate Management of Design*, London 1990

Mario Bellini/Olivetti, ETP 55 portable typewriter, 1987, plastics, metal

Dyson DC02 Vacuum Cleaner 1994-1995

James Dyson (1949)

Don't start by d
inside that's imp

James Dyson/Dyson, working prototype of the *DC 02*, 1992–1995, plastics, height 30 cm

igning the outside. it's what's

James Dyson/Dyson, working drawing of the DC 02, 1992-1995

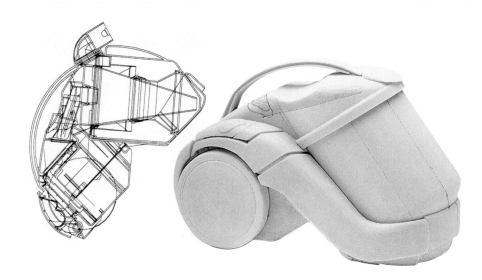

The first suction-based carpet cleaner was developed in 1901 by Hubert Cecil Booth, a British engineer who was known for his work designing fairground rides and mechanical exhibition installations. Booth's contraption was intended as a carpet cleaning service, with a machine so large it stayed in the street whilst hoses were taken from it into homes and offices. The first domestic vacuum cleaner, powered by electricity, was developed by an American janitor named James Murray Spangler in 1907. Spangler sold the rights to his invention to William Hoover, who founded the Hoover Suction Company in 1908, producing its first commercially successful lightweight Sweeper in 1909. Electrolux refined the principles of the vacuum cleaner in 1915 with the launch of its cylinder cleaner. The development of the vacuum cleaner was from then on primarily concerned with producing more lightweight and portable cleaners. The basic technology remained relatively unchanged until the late twentieth century, when James Dyson's challenge to the vacuum cleaner market turned the industry upside down.

Dyson's basic idea was to remove the bag from the standard suction cleaner, because it clogs with dust almost immediately, therefore seriously reducing suction power. In the late 1970s, faced with the problem of dust extraction at the factory set up to produce one of his other products – the Ballbarrow – Dyson constructed a giant cyclone chimney to extract the dust and powder by means of centrifugal force. The cyclone spins the dust out of the air, trapping the particles but allowing the air to escape. His first attempt was to construct a working prototype from cardboard and tape, attached to a traditional vacuum cleaner. It was this principle that he adapted as the basis for the Dual Cyclone (cleaner, fitting one cyclone inside another for greater efficiency (an eight-cyclone version was launched in 2002).

After a period of difficult business relations and with very little financial backing,

James Dyson/Dyson, *DC 02*, 1995, plastics, height 30 cm

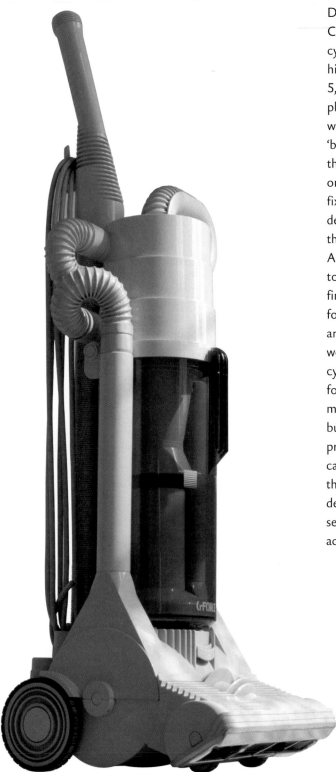

Dyson set up the Air Power Vacuum Cleaner Company at his home, where the cyclone was developed in a workshop. By his own estimation, Dyson made some 5,127 prototypes from cardboard, foam, plastic and metal. The three-dimensional working models are still referred to as 'breadboards' by the company, because this was the name of the plywood screen onto which the first prototypes were fixed. This hands-on approach to design development is still very much a part of the company's working method.

Although Dyson had originally intended to manufacture the product himself, financial difficulties prevented this and forced him instead to license his idea to another company. With one complete working prototype – a red and blue single-cyclone cleaner – together with the idea for a dual cyclone, Dyson approached major appliance manufacturers in Europe, but with little success. After a short-lived production run in the UK of 500 units called the Cyclon, Dyson took the idea to the US, where an unsuccessful licensing deal started a legal battle that lasted for several years and prevented any further activity in the US market. Finally in 1986, after a successful deal with the Japanese company Apex Inc., the G-Force Cyclonic Cleaner was launched on the Japanese market. The machine was manufactured to very high standards and because it came with a high price tag, it was inevitably a niche product that quickly acquired a reputation as a high-style designer product. Its distinctive design, plus the unusual story of a British designer selling successfully in the Japanese appliance market, garnered a great deal of publicity for Dyson in Europe.

Back in Britain, Dyson had returned to his original idea of designing and manufacturing products himself. A further period of development led to the completion of the Dyson Dual Cyclone DC01 in 1992, in grey and yellow plastic with a clear bin and extendable hose incorporated into the upright handle. The first production examples, manufactured in Wales, were ready the following year and sold initially through the mail-order catalogue network before being taken up by major electrical retailers. By mid-1993 Dyson had moved the tooling into his own premises and was running his own factory and research centre. Two years later, in 1995, the DC02 was launched, transforming the technology that was developed for an upright cleaner into a compact, cylinder version. Such a change to the form of the product was not straightforward, because a horizontal collection bin was in danger of leaking dust. The solution was to place the bin at an angle with a hinge for opening. The DC02 also has the capacity to 'sit' on a staircase whilst cleaning and even to 'climb' the stairs when pulled along. It has an anthropomorphic quality, so that it looks and behaves, as Dyson says, 'like a little domestic pet.' A year after its launch it was the best selling cylinder cleaner in the UK.

The philosophy of design and business as advocated by Dyson Appliances is bound up with the mythology of its product. The company employs a clear and consistent advertising slogan: 'We've said goodbye to the bag', but it also achieves a high profile media presence by its regular battles with rivals over claims of efficiency. Dyson's provocative entry into the market generated a high level of activity in a previously moribund product sector. As the public face of the company James Dyson has become well known as a spokesperson for British design, innovation and entrepreneurship. The identity of Dyson products is highly distinctive – employing a colour palette of pastel and acid colours that was rarely seen in the white, grey and beige world of domestic appliances. The products also all have a transparent plastic drum – ostensibly for functional reasons and for the 'pleasure' of seeing the results of one's labour. Dyson has also played on the self-conscious design appeal of its product by regularly launching limited edition models in different colour ranges. The 'De Stijl' DCO2 in 1996 paid homage to the Dutch design movement, and the 'Antarctica Solo' in the same year formed part of a charitable sponsorship.

Almost a decade on, characteristics like translucency, colour and anthropomorphism are commonplace in contemporary product design, due in no small part to the paradigm-shifting effects of companies such as Dyson and Apple. The company has branched out into other product areas, launching the Dyson CR01 washing machine in 2000. Dyson Appliances maintains that its design approach is about re-thinking, rather than re-styling the product.

Designer
and using
it look pr

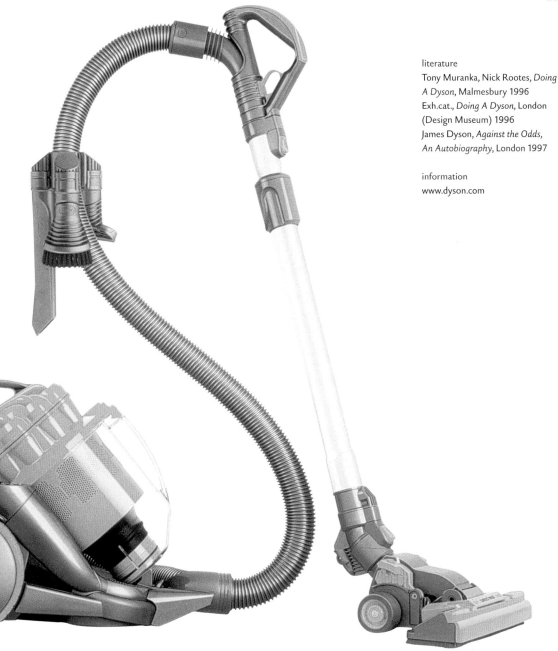

literature
Tony Muranka, Nick Rootes, *Doing A Dyson*, Malmesbury 1996
Exh.cat., *Doing A Dyson*, London (Design Museum) 1996
James Dyson, *Against the Odds, An Autobiography*, London 1997

information
www.dyson.com

hould be building, testing
he product, not just making
ty.

Stockman Collection
Spring-Summer 1997
Autumn-Winter 1997

Maison Martin Margiela
(founded 1988)

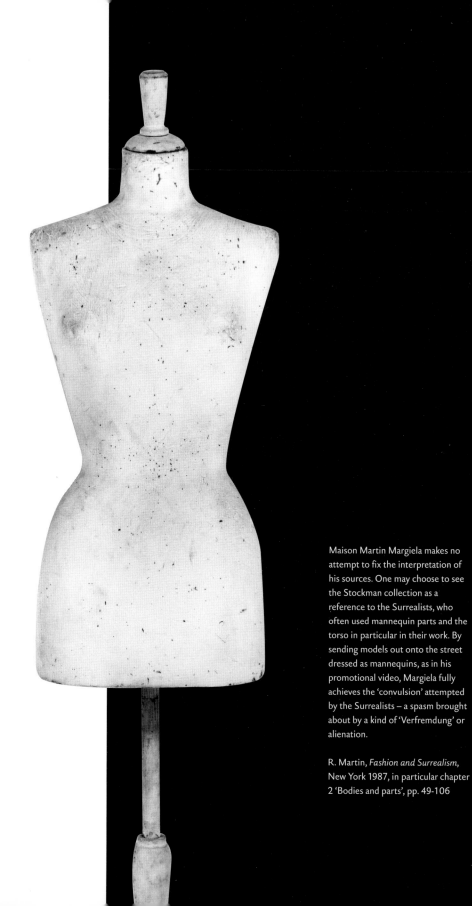

Maison Martin Margiela makes no attempt to fix the interpretation of his sources. One may choose to see the Stockman collection as a reference to the Surrealists, who often used mannequin parts and the torso in particular in their work. By sending models out onto the street dressed as mannequins, as in his promotional video, Margiela fully achieves the 'convulsion' attempted by the Surrealists – a spasm brought about by a kind of 'Verfremdung' or alienation.

R. Martin, *Fashion and Surrealism*, New York 1987, in particular chapter 2 'Bodies and parts', pp. 49-106

TENUE N° 8

- GILET-STOCKMAN
TL019/96153/23
- ETUDE D'UN COTE DE
DRAPE E97RBDRAP01
- JEANS
PL039/97510/82
- VESTE DOUBLE
BOUTONNAGE
GL045/98671/94 OU
GL046/98671/94

LE PANTALON EST PORTE
EN DESSOUS DU GILET,
PAR DESSUS L'ETUDE DE
DRAPE
CETTE TENUE PEUT ÊTRE
PORTEE AVEC OU SANS
VESTE

Spring 1997

Show-room
2 bis Passage Ruelle, 18de arrondissement, Paris
A white decor stands within the main area of the showroom space. A field of imitation sunflowers is planted in the floor. The sales of the collection as well as press meetings take place amid the flowers.

Presentation October 1996
A video showing two women wearing the collection walking through the streets and metro adjacent to the showroom, intercut with segments showing the production of pieces at our 'atelier'. A fax is sent to the hotels of the press inviting them to take an appointment at our showroom. The garments and themes of the collection are explained verbally, by video and on a showroom model who wears certain combinations of pieces of the collection. Light orchestral 'musak' plays throughout the space.

Collection
The first part of one collection for two seasons. The mould of a Tailor's dummy (or Dress form) in rough linen is a foundation for the collection. The object is worn directly on the skin, either with a slip skirt or a permanently dyed Blue Jeans. Various elements, from the varying stages of the development of a garment, are pinned to the Tailor's dummy form: shoulder pads, binding and garment studies. A simple unfinished square of fabric, a trial to examine the drape of a fabric, becomes a skirt or a dress with an irregular hem-line. Jackets are cut to a man's proportions. Once finished the internal structure of the prototype was removed and a second, feminine, shoulder line is added through the use of shoulder pads over which the original, man's shoulder line hangs. Studies for various parts of draped dresses in chiffon are worked by hand onto structures in elastic and corset bones, becoming garments in their own right. The soles of our shoes, mounted on heels, are worn on the feet.

Maison Martin Margiela, *Studio*

Autumn 1997

Show-room
2 bis Passage Ruelle, 18de arrondissement, Paris
A white decor, lit by many multi-coloured spotlights, stands within the
main area of the showroom.

Presentation March 1997
Many various types of free promotional maps of Paris are stamped with
the address one of the tree different locations: 10.30 hrs, LA JAVA, at
Belleville, an abandoned covered market 11.45 hrs, LE GIBUS, at République,
the glass covered loading bay of this huge building and, 15.00 hrs at
LA MENAGERIE DE VERRE, metro Parmentier, a 1930's dance school. A bus
carrying a 35 strong brass band leaves Brussels for Paris at 05.00 hrs to
meet another bus carrying the thirty-five models from the showroom to
their first destination. The band plays slow marching music at each
location. The invited crowd see the arrival of the buses. The third location,
Le Menagerie de Verre, is barely used as, at the last minute, it is decided
that the women wearing the collection walk amongst the waiting crowd in
the street.

Collection
The second part of the one collection for 1997-1998. The collection
comprises four series of garments and objects tracing the stages in the
production of a garment as well as reworked traditional garments. These
series are: 1/. Traditional structured garments, 2/. Garment studies,
3/. First fitting prototypes ('Toile'), 4/. Assembled garment patterns.
The mould of a Tailor's Dummy/Dress form remains a foundation. The
aims of the Dummy/Dress Form, in calico and linen, are added for winter.
Studies for coats show their internal structure. First fitting prototypes
('Toile') made in rough calico show all of their corrected faults and
instructions for adjustment. Garment patterns, assembled so that they may
be worn are made up in industrial untearable paper. As in the first part of
the collection in Summer, the coats and jackets are cut to man's
proportions. For the show they are worn as capes, their arms tucked inside.
Wigs in recycled fur are made up from old and used coats.

Since its foundation in 1988 Maison Martin Margiela has consistently broken every written and unwritten rule of fashion. Its creative director Martin Margiela escapes from every kind of mythologising and the allure of stardom by remaining entirely anonymous and communicating exclusively through and about his company's product: clothing. Averse to the conventions of producing a new collection each season, he re-uses successful old models, whereby his collections have the cumulative quality of an artist's oeuvre rather than the fleeting and modish nature of fashion. His love of and fidelity to proven models is expressed very literally in his re-use of old garments (recycling), his copying of second-hand items (reproduction) and the deployment of as many classical tailoring traditions as possible. This was very clearly displayed in his tenth and twentieth collections, in which the best products of the previous years were revived. An innovative element, usually a concept, forms the basis of a great variety of items of clothing. So, in the spring of 1993 he launched contrasting but identical black and white collections, in the autumn of 1995 a collection of photographed garments and in both the spring and autumn of 1997 collections centred on the genesis of a single item. The basis of the collections was the Stockman tailor's dummy, the stiff linen covering of which he presented as a universal silhouette, worn over tight jeans with exaggerated turn-ups. Haute couture draperies in three variants, paper patterns, fabric studies joined with tacking stitches, first fitting studies in unbleached cotton (toiles) and knitting samples served to bring the silhouettes to life.

Margiela's non-conformist approach found its ultimate expression in a radical presentation during his solo exhibition at Museum Boijmans Van Beuningen. Garments deliberately impregnated with various bacteria and fungi were exposed to the elements in the museum's garden. The exhibition was also shown in New York, Tokyo and Kyoto (1998-1999).

literature
Exh.cat., *Maison Martin Margiela, 9/4/1615*, Rotterdam (Museum Boijmans Van Beuningen) 1997
'Maison Martin Margiela', *Street*, Special edition, vol. 1&2, 1999

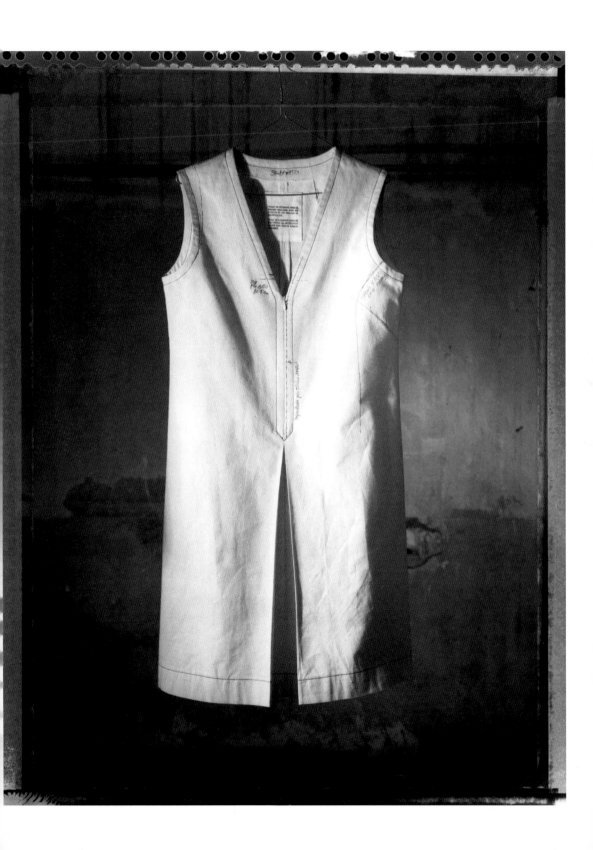

Haute Couture Collection
Autumn-Winter 1997-1998

John Galliano (1960)
Dior

Christian Dior, *Ligne Bar* outfit, 1947, silk and wool

The basis for each clothing design is a body – a drawn silhouette, a living model or a tailor's dummy – and then follows the fabric. That body is seldom perfect, but it is easily bedecked, adorned and wrapped in order to come closer to a perfect ideal. The highest achievement is *haute couture*, in which an exclusive design is made to measure for each individual client.

In the world of *haute couture* Paris occupies a unique position because of its strict rules governing the design process and the production standards of its fashion houses. The *couturier* must be 'of his time'. Twice a year he must comment on the period in which he lives, on beauty and on femininity through his collections, consisting of some hundred designs. But he – or she – must also provide a service for the few hundred women in the world who can afford to buy these creations. The image counts for the public, the materials for the individual.

One of the rules of *couture* is that each design must be produced especially for a single client, tailored to her unique figure. Firstly in the form of a *toile* – a heavy cotton model to which alterations can be made – and then in the real, often costly, fabrics. This sets *couture* apart from ready-to-wear, even the luxury off-the-peg creations to which a 'designer' gives his or her name. Each piece of *couture* is unique; ready-to-wear is reproducible. Nowadays *couture* and ready-to-wear are often part of a single brand name – a fashion house with a special, distinct style that is immediately recognisable in the smallest details. Amongst the most special of these is the House of Dior.

Christian Dior's individual style has been fiercely guarded, allowing his name to live on long after his death in 1957. The foundations that he laid in the extraordinarily successful 'Ligne Corolle' in 1947, which made international headlines as the 'New Look', are still visible in each collection.

But there is more: the House of Dior also represents an image of femininity that distinguishes it from other houses such as Chanel or Yves Saint Laurent. The Chanel woman is *sportif*, elegant and energetic; her counterpart at YSL is entirely aware of her feminine wiles – simultaneously unapproachable and vulnerable.

The House of Dior has twice set in motion a revolution through this image of femininity. The first was in 1947, when the end of the War was marked with the introduction of the New Look. The second, almost fifty years later, in 1997, when the Englishman John Galliano turned the chic fashion house into a twice-yearly 'house party' by sampling the entire history of fashion like a DJ.

House by Dior

Both events created an international furore and both ensured enormous commercial success. With one major difference: in the months following the launch of the New Look every fashion-conscious woman sat behind a sewing-machine making her own version of the long, wide skirt. Galliano's *début* as creative director at Dior resulted instead in increased sales of cosmetics, the medium through which his extraordinary first collection made reference to the Masai and 1930s *chinoiserie*. The material versus the virtual – is how one may sum up the developments of the last fifty years.

Couture at the beginning of the twenty-first century is a remarkable business. The time is now gone when a single designer was able to stamp his mark on a particular season's 'street-style'. And it is possibly precisely because this glory period is no more – but nonetheless many women once again desire the exclusivity of a unique outfit with the aura of a work of art – that *couture* has blossomed so fully in the last few years.

At Dior she
is sensual and
seductive:
the essence
of a woman.

René Gruau, sketch for *Ligne Envol* outfit, Christian Dior, 1948

he New Look made such an enormous impact because extravagance was so provocative in 1947, so soon after the second World War. And there was extravagance in abundance at Dior: an excess of fabrics, a voluptuousness of rounded forms – breasts and hips – and an embarassment of feminine chic – accessories such as high heels, a handbag, gloves, costume jewellery and a hat were essential to the effect of the New Look. It was all too irresistible after a period of such scarcity. Christian Dior brought about a renewal of sensuality, which was to become synonymous with his name from that moment on. He fashioned an ode to femininity, inspired by and in admiration of his chic mother. The essence of this sensuality was the silhouette; the nipped-in waistline contrasting with the long, wide, flared skirt and the jacket cut tightly round full breasts and slender arms. This silhouette was the result of a precise construction of the individual elements of the garments. This physical perfectionism, or at least the appearance of it, could be achieved only by moulding a preformed figure in the material with darts, reinforcements and padding.

John Galliano took this constructed feminity as his starting point. His arrival at Dior followed a turbulent career, firstly in London, where his degree show Les Incroyables received immediate and unprecedented attention for his reinterpretation of the clothing of the French Revolution; and thereafter with his combination of image and craftsmanship (biascut evening dresses) in collections that he made for a select group of wealthy, cosmopolitan women, who assembled in

John Galliano/Dior, QE II outfit, spring/summer 1998, woollen crêpe

John Galliano/Dior, *Fashion show*, autumn/winter 1997–1998

Paris each year especially for his shows. Galliano did not design for *his* mother. He designed for the avant-garde jet-set. He belonged in the 1980s to the fashion crowd that incorporated within their collections influences from London's and New York's exciting street culture and nightlife. Pop music accompanied each design. Designers unleashed a fashion revolution against which French couture had no defences. Dior had been headed since 1990 by the stylish, but elderly Gianfranco Ferrè, so it was something of a culture shock when Dior brought in the young Galliano.

literature
Colin McDowell, *Galliano*, London 1997

uddenly Dior's extravagance was given a new, contemporary, neaning. Galliano appropriated the extravagance of the twentieth entury's richest imagery, coupling the street with the salon. He ansacked every image from his limitless fantasies, his knowledge of ther cultures and the entire history of art in innovative collections; ut never lost sight of the physicality and sensuality that the House f Dior had patented. He also follows a simple, but unbreakable rule: Dior woman always has a waist. And the waist forms the start of ach elegant movement.

Ford Concept Car 021C
1999

Marc Newson (1963)

PANTONE Warm Red C

PANTONE Orange 021 C

PANTONE Yellow 012 C

PANTONE Yellow C

Marc Newson/Ford Motor Company, model of the Ford Concept car 021C, side view, 1999

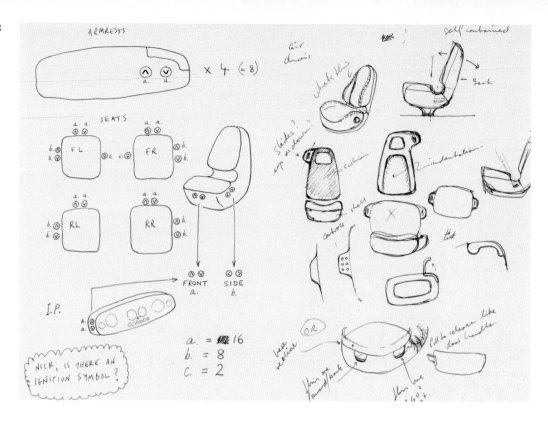

Marc Newson, sketch of the seats of the *Ford Concept car 021C*, 1999, ballpoint ink on paper

The Ford Motor Company's decision to ask the London-based, Australian product and interior designer, Marc Newson, to create a radically 'different' car for the 1999 Tokyo Motor Show can be seen as a continuation of the twentieth-century tradition in which the skills of designers known for their successful industrial products – Norman Bel Geddes and Raymond Loewy among them – were applied to the 'problem of the automobile' with stunning results. Born in Sydney in 1963 Newson had studied sculpture and jewellery; lived and worked as a designer in Japan and Paris; established himself as a product designer of some repute (with clients including Alessi, Cappellini, and Flos); and created interior spaces for shops and restaurants such as Belgium's W&LT, New York's Canteen and Tokyo's Pod Bar before Ford approached him with the car project.

In the heroic tradition of Harley Earl's dramatic creations for General Motors in the 1950s the 021C (the name came from the pantone code for the shade of orange that was used for the Tokyo model) was conceived as a 'concept car' – i.e., one which was not itself destined for mass production but which was used to communicate new ideas and applications of advanced technologies. Unlike Earl's sci-fi-inspired monsters, however, Newson's turn-of-the-century design set out to rethink the design of the motor car from scratch. Rather than to perpetuate the meaning of the automobile as a symbol of power, sexuality and social status he aimed to exploit all that modern materials and technologies could offer in the task of creating a functional artefact which could carry its passengers from A to B in an efficient, user-friendly manner.

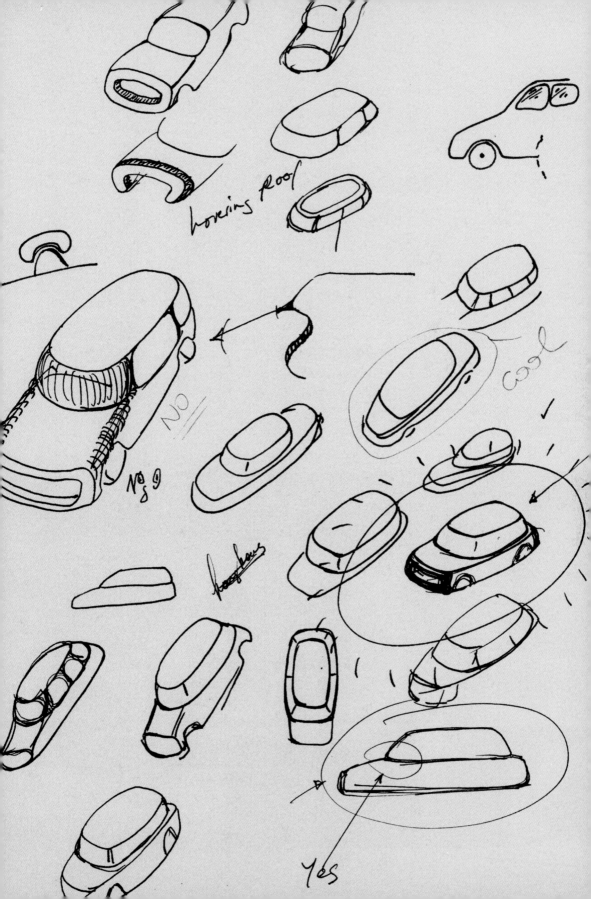

hovering Roof

NO///

N°9

cool

Yes

Although Newson took nothing for granted, some things, he decided, could stay. The familiar profile created by the combination of the covered engine in the front, the covered space for the driver and passengers in the middle and the covered boot for luggage in the rear, for example, was retained. In contrast to the visual excesses of much automobile styling, however, the basic form of the 021C is simple, unelaborated and, above all, non-aggressive. Most of the car's familiar details were reworked. In the boot, for example, Newson addressed the long-term problem of lifting heavy luggage in and out by providing a large tray that slid out automatically. In order to provide sufficient space in the boot he ensured that the layout of the rear suspension was compact.

Spaciousness and easy accessibility feature strongly in the middle section of the 021C as well. Here Newson has made it possible for both the front and rear doors to open from the centre and to eliminate a central column which would impede access. His description of the interior as, 'a great big bath tub with everything floating' expresses his strong desire to get away from the bulky, fixed elements which characterise the conventional car and which make its interior space problematic. His aircraft-style seats, which pivot on pedestals for easy movement, go a long way

Marc Newson for Ford Motor Company, model of the Ford Concept car 021C, side view, 1999

towards alleviating this. Many of the interior's technological features derive from Newson's experience as a product designer: The roof, for example, is lined with electro-luminescent lights, usually found in watches and calculators, and the dials on the dashboard were made by Ike, a Swiss watch manufacturer with whom Newson has collaborated on the creation of what were called his 'Ikepod' watches. An innovative use of illumination plays an important role in the 021C: Not only do the door handles – simple aluminium buttons surrounded by Perspex rings – light up when the remote control locking is activated, the Ford logo is illuminated when the headlights are turned on. The

Marc Newson/Ford Motor Company, model of the *Ford Concept car 021C*, front view, 1999

Marc Newson/Ford Motor Company, model of the *Ford Concept car 021C*, interior, 1999

headlights themselves are made of LED and fibre optic strips that can be used in broad bands.

The decision to use push buttons and watch-inspired technology was an intrinsic part of Newson's general strategy, which was to redefine the car as a functional product rather than fantasy fulfilment. The form of the rubber-covered, moulded fibre-glass steering wheel, for instance, was developed from a coat-hook that the designer was working on for Alessi and the 'eyeball' mechanism of the small joy-stick situated on the centre of the dashboard was borrowed from aeroplane air-conditioning units.

In the construction of the 021C, however, Newson exploited the traditional methods used by car stylists for nearly a century. A half-size clay model was followed by the creation of two full-size ones – for the interior and the exterior – which permitted the designer to understand the real spaces involved and to see the way in which light falls onto surface of the body. At this point new production technologies were introduced and CAD software, linked to a milling machine, was used to create the final model. The carbon fibre components that emerged from GRP moulds were built around a steel framework and the internal mechanics, the windows and the paint finishes were subsequently added to create the complete model. The result is a car that is conceptually radical. Newson's attention to detail (even the hourglass pattern on the surface of the tyres is repeated on the interior carpet, woven in silk especially for this project), his commitment to new materials and technologies, his transfer of knowledge from one design arena to another and his redefinition of the car as a functional product for the here and now, rather than a fantasy which can never be fulfilled, have combined to create a model for the car of the twenty-first century.

information
www.marc-newson.com

Marc Newson/Ikepod Watch Co, *Hemipode watch*, 1996, metaal en rubber

Air Chair 1997-1999

Jasper Morrison (1959)

The manufacture of Jasper Morrison's Air Chair conforms to a modernist fantasy in which perfectly formed identical products are ejected from a machine continuously. There are no parts to assemble; each emerges complete and whole. There is no original model; each is an exact replica of the others made before it and those that will succeed it. At the moment of extraction from the mould, each is unblemished, timeless, ageless and untouched. It is without history, and beyond style. It represents the summation of a design and manufacturing process deriving high-productivity from mass-production in the service of mass-consumption. It is a cheap, efficient process resulting in affordable, functional products.

Utopian? Well, yes and no. The quest for such pure products informed the modernist experiment throughout the twentieth century (and, in different manners, earlier in the industrial revolution that transformed the manufacturing and consumption of goods). Plastic was (and remains) the most 'modern' of all materials, not only because of its ability to be anything but because of its resistance to 'craft' techniques and its insistence on industrial processes. Early pioneers of plastic used synthetic compounds to cheaply replicate expensive materials, but by the mid-twentieth century plastic was celebrated for its own virtues, namely its affordability and malleability.

While appearing to offer both the manufacturer and the consumer unlimited choice and possibilities, plastic products became the victim of their own ubiquity and synthetic nature. They were perfect simulacra of something intrinsically more

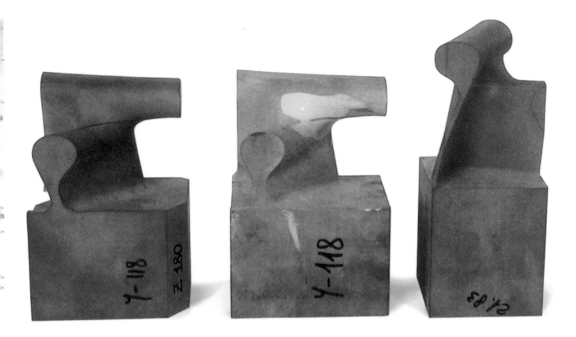

valuable, and as a result debased themselves and the original source. Environ-mentalism and global politics further devalued oil-based plastics in the 1970s.

For furniture designers and manufacturers, however, the quest for the perfect one-piece moulded chair has been continuous for half a century or more. Working in plywood, 1930s pioneers such as Gerald Summers and Alvar Aalto began to fulfil the ideal, followed by Eames, Panton and others using new post-war plastics and fibreglass. The attraction of manufacturing moulded furniture is that it is a fast and efficient substitute for time-consuming assembly processes. Although the invest-ment in research and tooling is very high, manufacturers hope to reap profits from the sheer volume of low-cost units they can make. It was not until the 1960s, how-ever, that moulded plastic chairs were a technical reality, and then many of them were deceptive in that they were often composites of components.

The success of injection-moulded furniture relied on the addition of thickness and ribs to stress-bearing elements of a design to give the chair structural stability. Designers like Magistretti and Columbo made virtues of the structural ribs in their furniture, incorporating them into the aesthetic of the object in much the same way as High-Tech architecture wears its services with pride. A certain honesty of design informs these objects: they are highly engineered and seem so.

Not so the Air Chair, which is the closest we have come to achieving the modernist grail of the single-moulded chair. There is no visible structure, just pure surface stretched out in the shape of a chair. Its lines are as fluid as the polypropylene that

Morrison recalls the design process:
'Design and prototyping was fairly quick, with
unusually few changes made to the first prototype.
I think we had defined the shape within about nine
months of the start of the project. Mould making
and designing of the mould to position gas and
plastic injection points (separate) took a while longer,
followed by test mouldings to balance everything
(mould temperatures, mould cycle times, cooling
areas) and get a good result. It was probably two
years altogether.'

Correspondence with the author, January 2003

enters the mould. Its simplicity (no joins, no struts, no upholstery, no obvious *moulding*) makes it close to being an ideal made real; a representation of a chair. It could only be made of plastic, which Roland Barthes observed could be used to manufacture anything, 'buckets as well as jewels'. For Barthes plastic is, 'ubiquity made visible' and, 'less a thing than a trace of a movement', being the miraculous process of its production.[1]

It takes just four minutes to make an Air Chair and its near-instantaneous appearance from a single mould solidifies the plastic at a moment in time.
The Air Chair's success as a design derives from the gas-injection technology that is used to manufacture it. Gas injection internalises all structural forces within the body of the plastic itself. There is no need for visible struts and braces. The technology relies on advanced computer modelling which can identify and calculate the stresses within the design of the chair long before the tooling is made. Alone, the polypropylene is too flexible to create the chair so, before moulding, it is

1
Exh.cat.,
*The Plastics Age.
From Modernity
to Postmodernity,*
London (Victoria
& Albert
Museum) 1990,
pp. 11-111

mixed with fibreglass to add strength. As the liquid mixture is injected into the mould air pockets are introduced in a finely tuned procedure. Morrison relates this highly technological process back to natural principles by describing the chair as, 'like a bone, hollow in the middle'.[2] The air pockets not only displace areas of plastic, making the chair more economical to manufacture and lighter to use, but the solid sections between the voids of the air channels act as skeletal ribs. It is a reductive process rather than an act of addition. The chair's mass is affected by the air pockets, leaving thicker, stronger areas where stresses are most intense and thinner, lighter areas where the stresses are less intense. The air chambers are integral to the body of the chair, and here the skeletal analogy ends, because the surface is the same material as the structure supporting it. The speed, temperature, pressure and direction of the liquid polypropylene's injection into the mould also affect the stress balance, and this too can be calculated virtually.

Morrison's client for the Air Chair was the design-led Italian manufacturer Magis, which had already built a reputation for products celebrating and advancing the use of plastics. It was Magis that suggested a lightweight single-piece plastic chair, and which proposed the used of gas-injection moulding, a technology developed for the production of car components such as door fascias.

The Air Chair was launched to great critical acclaim in 2000. Subsequently Magis has developed the Air range by adding tables and a trolley, sharing the technology and a familial appearance with the chair. In 2003 Morrison and Magis are developing a folding Air Chair intended for a different market sector to that of the original chair. Two years in gestation, four minutes in creation, 200,000 now produced, world-wide distribution and rock-bottom prices; the Air Chair comes close to fulfilling modernism's fantasy.

[2]
Correspondence with the author, January 2003

literature
S. Katz, Classic Plastics. From Bakelite to High-Tech, London 1984
Exh.cat., The Plastics Age. From Modernity to Postmodernity, London (Victoria & Albert Museum) 1990
J. Meikle, American Plastic. A Cultural History, New Brunswick 1995
J. Morrison, A World Without Words, Baden 1998
C.A. Boyer, F. Zanco, Jasper Morrison, Paris 1999
C. Lefteri, Plastic. Material for Inspirational Design, Crans-Près-Céligne 2001
J. Morrison, Everything but the Walls, Baden 2002

Jasper Morrison /Magis, four stacked *Air Chairs*, 1999, polypropylene with fibreglass

My Soft Office 2000

Hella Jongerius (1962)

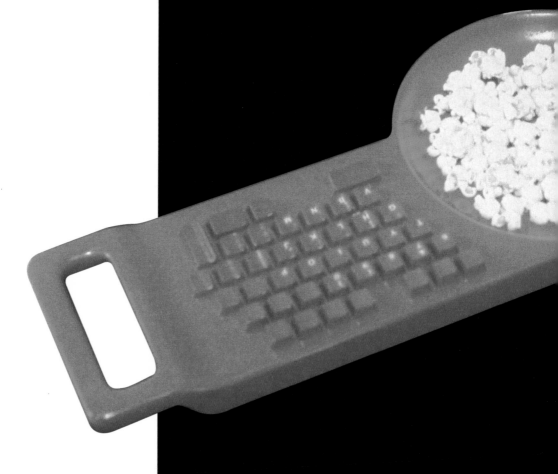

Hella Jongerius/Jongerius Lab, Weekly dinner, 2000, painted MDF, length 64 cm

The designs of Hella Jongerius often teeter on the brink between idea and product. Usually they are materialised thoughts and visions. They make one think, which is their distinctive quality. They open the mind and dust away the cobwebs of ideas. Her input for companies often lies in the continuation of that, realising renewal from the rich past, developing products with a twist. Her vision of computer use in the home environment was given form in a presentation at the Museum of Modern Art in New York in 2000.

The Dutch designer – working the seams between craft and art, past and present – explores the industrialised one-off.

Jennifer Kabat, *Metropolis*, July 2002, p. 109

My Soft Office

'Home is where the heart is.' However, the heart is very often not where it feels at home, for example at work or in far-off virtual worlds. For the twenty-first century person the worlds of private and public, living and working are no longer strictly divided. However, you would not think that were the case if you tried to mix and match their attendant products. The successful marriage of homeliness and technical ingenuity is only to be found in the kitchen.

When the first computers gingerly entered our houses, they were immediately banished to the least cosy corner. And although their use has increased dramatically, from looking up cooking recipes to playing Nintendo, from keeping abreast of the share indexes to communicating professionally with the world, they still often lead an isolated existence amongst the bookcases. That has much to do with their design, which has remained scandalously behind the times. Only the computer giant Apple has successfully managed to blend the computer with the home with its hip, multicoloured I-Mac design. The other computers continue, with their overly boring design, to remind us too much of characterless office spaces. The time is ripe for a take-over bid.

Commissioned by the Museum of Modern Art in New York, the industrial designer Hella Jongerius finally reconciled living and working, sleeping and surfing the net, lazing by the fireside and looking up the temptations of the world outside. It resulted in a number of comfortable and attractive fashion objects that contain high-quality technology. She called it MY SOFT OFFICE. In her work Jongerius rarely goes in search of the umpteenth unique form, and so in her 'Bed in Business' she used archetypal references to domesticity: the bed, textiles and cushions. Large computer screens are incorporated into the end of the bed, and the keyboard and mouse within the 'touchpillows'.

The computer screen and keyboard also lurk within another design, the so-called 'Power Patches'; exceedingly comfortable cushions that lie spread over the floor waiting to be used. Here Jongerius did not seek an archetypal form, but stretched the limits still further: in these compact seating elements the busy and the relaxed make an agreeable treaty.

The patches contain a non-hardening gel through which comfort remains assured. By producing them in various materials each is invested with its own individual identity and atmosphere, from romantically classical to starkly modern. The fashionable patches seductively invite one to sit/recline/work.

Louise Schouwenberg, *Frame*, October 2000

New York revisited

The presentation in New York takes on a new form in Museum Boijmans Van Beuningen. In seeking an overarching metaphor for the work of the talented young Rotterdam-based designers, the museum chose the laboratory, in which research is more important than results. The replacement of Charles and Ray Eames' lounge version of working by Archizoom's chair 'Mies' gives it a more manifest character and the French designer-stylist Philippe Starck is substituted by the Belgian minimalist Maarten van Severen.

information
www.jongeriuslab.nl

Hella Jongerius/JongeriusLab, installation of *My Soft Office* at the Museum of Modern Art, New York, 2000

Warty tubes, with strangely fluid branchings poking out of them, or garned rings of frozen gunk with tumor-like excrescences.

Blake Godnik, *The Washington Post*, 21 April 2002

An almost otherworldly little thing that even the most confused mind could not have conceived.

W.P. Paul Hartman, 'Gezinsgewijs sinteren', *Product, tijdschrift voor productontwikkeling*, September 2001, pp. 38-40

Marcel Wanders (1963)

The Airborne Snotty Vase 2001

Marcel Wanders/Cappellini, *the Airborne Snotty Vase, Coryza*, 2001, polyamide, height 15 cm

The examination of Marcel Wanders' oeuvre with a magnifying glass reveals time and again a single constant – the combination of high and low. Wanders' international breakthrough followed quickly when he combined hypermodern plastic-reinforced carbon fibre with the most craftsy technique imaginable: macramé. From this handknotting that was used in the 1970s for amateur wall-hangings, bags and waistcoats, he constructed a feather-light chair – the Knotted Chair from 1996 – which is the envy of many an engineer.

Since Cappelini, one of the world's leading manufacturers, added the chair to its collection this Dutch designer has rocketed to the stars. His lamp subsequently designed for the lighting manufacturer Flos, a sconce with a candle shape bulp, contains a technical novum: there is no on/off switch, you simply blow out the candle with a small puff of air. One of the most bizarre products to sprout from Wanders' unbridled creative mind is the Airborn Snotty Vase, which is also distributed by Cappellini. Wanders combined a miniscule glob of snot with the ultramodern laser-driven rapid prototyping process to produce a vase that looks like it has come from another planet. He got five people with different nasal complaints to sneeze into a modern 3-D scanner. A sophisticated computer program transformed them into three-dimensional models, from which a vase was produced – a thousand-times enlarged –from a pile of powder by a laser. Whoever sets this spatial monstrosity on their table will have a conversation piece for years to come.

Nano-technology is used here as a craft technique, but the process is too expensive to allow the vases to be mass produced; the works are like laboratory toys, thy molecules blown up to nursery-sized playthings. In exploring disease Wanders finds a means of realizing it as an object – a vase.

Lorna Lee Leslie, 'A Breath of Fresh Air', *Frieze*, August 2001, pp. 76-77

information
www.marcelwanders.com

The Making of the Airborne Snotty Vase

We create miracles every day

Diseases of the nasal cavity

Ozaena
A discharge of fetid matter from the nostril, particulary if associated with ulceration of the soft parts and disease of the bones of the nose.

Influenza
An acute viral infection involving the respiratory tract, occurring in isolated cases, in epidemics or in pandemics striking many continents simultaneously or in sequence. It is marked by inflammation of the nasal mucosa, the pharynx and conjunctiva and by headache and severe, often generalised myalgia. Fever, chills and prostration are common.

Pollinosis
An inflammatory response in the nasal passages to an allergic stimulus. Often includes: nasal congestion, sneesing, runny or itchy nose. Also known as Hay fever.

Sinusitis
Inflammation of a sinus. The condition may be purulent or nonpurulent, acute or chronic. Depending on the site of involvement it is known as ethmoid, frontal, maxillary or sphenoid sinusitis.

Coryza
A runny nose. The word coryza came from the Greek koryza thought to have been compounded from kara, head + zeein, to boil = boiling over from the head.

A digital 3D nano-scan of a snotty

1 Prototype of a new micro-tech advanced scanning-device.
Especially engeneered to scan on micro-tech based level.
This makes it possible to scan the density of micoscopic objects.

2 Ozaena patient preparing to sneeze into the scanning-device.

3 Out of the whole 'rain' of particles one particle is selected and transferred by a 8 bit/rate processor to a computer device.

4 Ozaena identified.
Advanced 'IFN' softwareprogram which translates captured organic substances into computermodels.
Model editing and creating special design solutions.

5 The generated computermesh will be sent to the SLS-machine to produce a unique model of the captured particle.
Ozaena generated.

The production of the final 3D object

6 This machine produces the final object using 3D-drawing.
The model is build up by the computer guided laser.

THE MAKING OF...

THE *AIRBORNE SNOTTY VASE*
DESIGNED BY
mɘrcel wɘnders

concept and design . marcel wanders
marcel wanders · karin krautgartner

mesh modification · willem derks
graphic design booklet · vivian neeskens
selective laser sintering · amidox

cappellini   via marconi 35 22060 arosio italy

mɘrcel wɘnders

cappellini

© 2001, marcel wanders°, amsterdam

WE CREATE MIRACLES EVERY DAY

DISEASES OF THE NASAL CAVITY

Ozaena
A discharge of fetid matter from the nostril, particularly if associated with ulceration of the soft parts and disease of the bones of the nose

Coryza
A runny nose. The word coryza came from the Greek koryza thought to have been compounded from kara , head + zeein , to boil = boiling over from the head

Pollinosis
An inflammatory response in the nasal passages to an allergic stimulus. Often includes: nasal congestion, sneesing, runny or itchy nose. Also known as Hay fever.

Influenza
An acute viral infection involving the respiratory tract, occurring in isolated cases, in epidemics or in pandemics striking many continents simultaneously or in sequence. It is marked by inflammation of the nasal mucosa, the pharynx and conjunctive and by headache and severe, often generalised myalgia. Fever, chills and prostration are common.

Sinusitis
Inflammation of a sinus. The condition may be purulent or nonpurulent, acute or chronic. Depending on the site of involvement it is known as ethmoid, frontal, maxillary or sphenoid sinusitis.

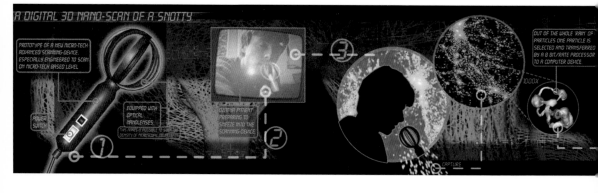

A DIGITAL 3D NANO-SCAN OF A SNOTTY

PROTOTYPE OF A NEW MICRO-TECH ADVANCED SCANNING-DEVICE. ESPECIALLY ENGINEERED TO SCAN ON MICRO-TECH BASED LEVEL

OUT OF THE WHOLE 'RAIN' OF PARTICLES ONE PARTICLE IS SELECTED AND TRANSFERRED BY A 8 BIT/RATE PROCESSOR TO A COMPUTER DEVICE.

EQUIPPED WITH OPTICAL NANOLENSES

THIS MAKES IT POSSIBLE TO SEE DENSITY OF MICROSCOPIC DEVICES

POWER SWITCH

OZAENA PATIENT PREPARING TO SNEEZE INTO THE SCANNING-DEVICE

1000X

CAPTURE

1   2   3

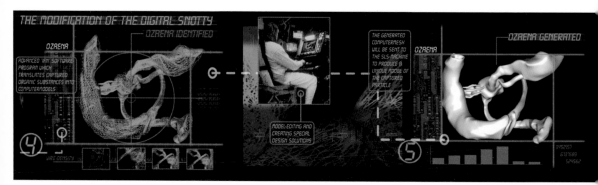

THE MODIFICATION OF THE DIGITAL SNOTTY

OZAENA IDENTIFIED

OZAENA GENERATED

OZAENA

ADVANCED 'IAA' SOFTWARE PROGRAM WHICH TRANSLATES CAPTURED ORGANIC SUBSTANCES INTO COMPUTERMODELS

THE GENERATED COMPUTERMESH WILL BE SENT TO THE SLS-MACHINE TO PRODUCE A UNIQUE MODEL OF THE CAPTURED PARTICLE

OZAENA

MODEL-EDITING AND CREATING SPECIAL DESIGN SOLUTIONS

4   WIRE DENSITY

5

3452157
6131683
524562

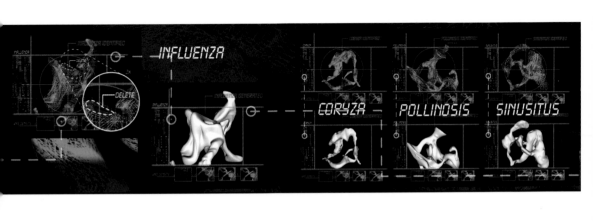

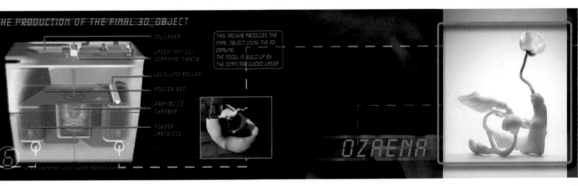

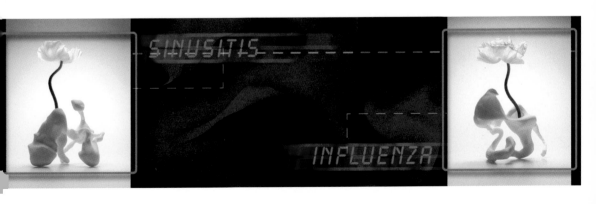

Prada New York
1999-2001

OMA
(founded 1975)

OMA
The Office for Metropolitan Architecture (OMA) is concerned with contemporary architecture, urbanism and general cultural issues. Founded in 1975 ar

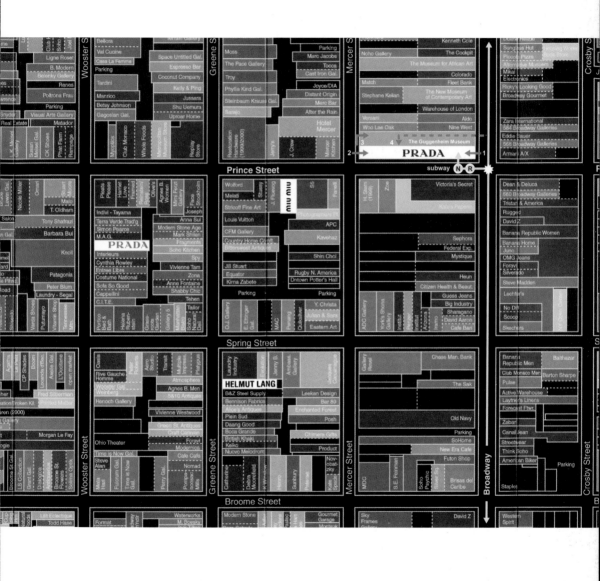

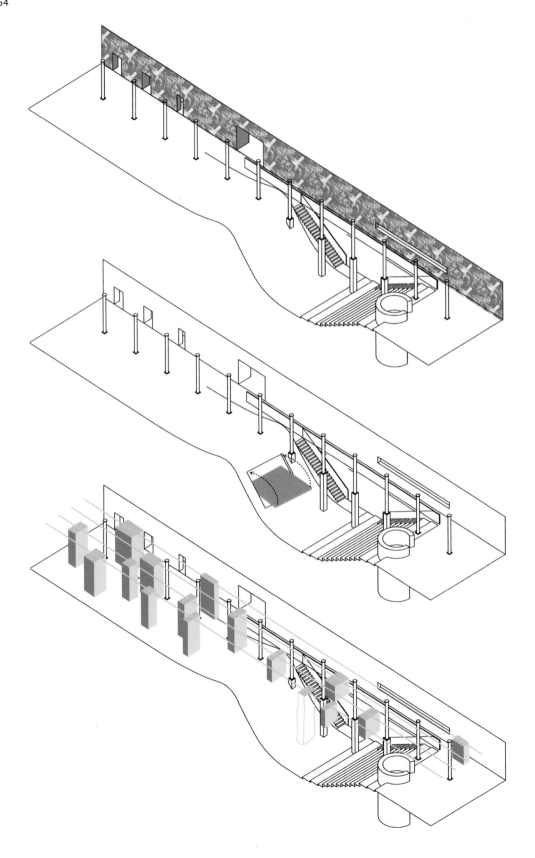

Rem Koolhaas/OMA, axonometric of *Prada New York*, wallpaper, podium, hanging city, 1999–2001

Rem Koolhaas/OMA, elevation of Prada New York, stairs and podium, 1999–2001

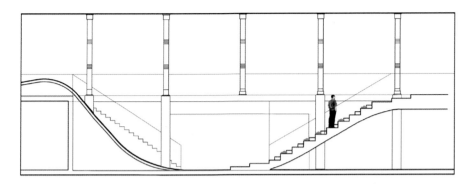

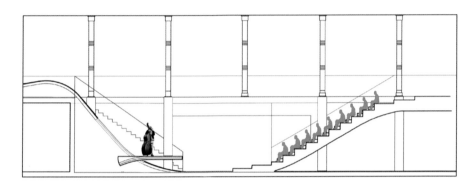

Located at the corner of Prince street and Broadway in New York city, the first Prada epicenter opened to the public on December 15, 2001. Prada in collaboration with Rem Koolhaas and the Office for Metropolitan Architecture (OMA) conceived the new store as a laboratory where the company can experiment with new forms of customer interaction.

In 1999 Prada commissioned OMA for a two-month research project that examined different ways in which they could reinvent their retail experience. Prada's dramatic growth required new strategies.

Scale alone seemed to demand an inevitable commercialization and endless repetition could alienate the very customers that made them so successful in the first place: customers who gravitated to Prada's position on the edge of Italian fashion culture and supported experimentation in design and materials.

That initial research project grew into the commission for the design of three big stores or epicenters, to be located in New York, Los Angeles, and San Francisco. (A fourth epicenter in Tokyo was designed by the Swiss architects Herzog & de Meuron.) The epicenters provide locations of concentrated creativity while Prada's familiar green boutiques will continue to stand as familiar outposts. The green

stores provide a consistent image, while the scale and strategic placement of the epicenter stores allow them to accommodate more product, more variation and to be site specific.

At the heart of the epicenter concept is the notion that Prada should perpetually reshape, rather than enshrine, their image. In the new stores Prada could transcend shopping and engage public space and cultural programming. The New York epicenter spans a spectrum from the Public to the ultra-Private; the design of the store allows those boundaries to constantly shift.

As the design of the New York store took shape, the development of in-store technology and content was taken on by OMA's alter-studio AMO. (AMO is a separate entity established by OMA to explore concepts beyond the traditional reach of architecture.) AMO, in conjunction with an international team of consultants – including

IDEO London and IconNicholson – developed an integrated array of custom in-store technologies, a content database, and a prototype Web site that will link the epicenter to the Internet.

The Prada New York epicenter is a working experiment. The space is designed to support new forms of customer service, merchandising, and programming. It is a space that enables change: change in the configuration of the store itself, its surfaces, its function, the content on the display devices, and the way customers are serviced. It is a place, ultimately, where Prada can experiment with new conditions and continuously reinvent itself.

The New York store occupies the ground floor of one building as well as the basement of the building next door. These two parallel, but misaligned, spaces were connected by only a small section of basement.

Rem Koolhaas/OMA, Prada New York, interior of the salesroom, 2001

Rem Koolhaas/OMA, *Prada New York, hanging city*, 2001

This condition spurred the central design gesture, a wave that manipulates the main floor of the space. Starting at Prince street, large steps descend to the lower level: the trough forms the connecting element that unites the street level with the basement. The presence of the wave, formed from a continuous surface of zebrawood flooring, creates a series of spaces: entry hall, stepped shoe display/seating, stage and the display area towards Mercer Street.

The wave creates an open space that can support a variety of program. The ascending part conceals an event platform within it, which unfolds mechanically. The shoe-display steps provide an auditorium for up to 200 people. Prada and the Prada Foundation have planned a number of cultural activities – from film programs and lectures to performance series – which will be hosted within the store.

The merchandise throughout the ground floor is displayed in moveable volumes. This 'hanging city' consists of a series of aluminum-mesh cages suspended from the ceiling which are configured to include hanging bars, shelving, and space for mannequins and other displays. The units are mounted on motorized tracks that allow them to be positioned differently throughout the store like inverted buildings or shopping addresses on a street. During events on the wave stage, the hanging city can be gathered together in a concentrated block at the back of the store, freeing the space for other activities.

A polycarbonate wall covers the original brick wall on the south side of the building and frames the main space. This translucent material blurs the existing conditions behind it: a pastiche of SoHo brick, construction markings, and original windows. The north wall is covered with custom wallpaper: its first manifestation is an enormous pattern of fragmented photographs. The theme and colors of the wallpaper will change with the seasons, providing both variety and an element of temporality. The entrance is dominated by the presence of a cylindrical glass elevator that provides access to the floor below. The 12-foot diameter cab contains a display of Prada handbags allowing patrons to shop as they descend to the lounge and accessories area in the basement. In this lounge customers can browse bags and leather goods while seated on plywood banquettes covered with gel pads. The main dressing rooms of the store are behind a wall of Privalit Glass that switches from translucent

Rem Koolhaas/OMA, Prada New York, stairs, 2001

to transparent. A black-and-white marble floor references the original Prada store in the Milan Galleria.

The lower level also includes a cosmetics display area, designed by the Japanese architect Kazuyo Sejima, more shoe displays, and a series of rooms formed by customized compact shelving units of the type used in libraries. These units can be combined or separated to create different special conditions depending on the volume of merchandise. They provide the sense that the customer is shopping behind-the-scenes in an environment part-storage and part-display.

As AMO set out to explore the way technology would be integrated in the new epi-centers, a number of key concepts were established: Be unobtrusive, integrated, and functional; Support, rather than change, existing ways of working; Help provide better service; Build on interactions and relationships in the real world.

AMO worked under the basic premise that content and imagery should not be contrived or 'branded' but rather be an explicit representation of the company in all its richness, complexity, adventure and contradiction, showing it as a compelling entity in its own right and as part of a larger cultural context.

At the center of the technology-based service scenario is a staff device developed together with IDEO London and IconNicholson. The handheld wireless store data-base terminal gives the salesperson up-to-date access to inventory and customer information.

In addition, the staff device serves as a interface for other elements in the service scenario: reading radio frequency identification (RFID) tags that identify products, staff, and customers via a personalized customer card. The device also controls video displays throughout the store.

Information from the staff device can be displayed on any of the various screens in

the store and so shared with the customer. When not employed as service terminals, those screens (called ubiquitous displays) exhibit other content – video, graphic material, computational information – and can be placed with merchandise on hang-bars, on table tops or in display furniture creating changing contexts for the products – supporting and challenging them. A unique database system allows such content to be extremely diverse, easily changed or reprogrammed. In addition there are three specialized media booths that provide sites for other forms of audio-visual experimentation.

In the dressing rooms service information is directly accessible to the customer. Any article the customer places into the closet is registered automatically and displayed on the closet touch screen. From that screen, the customer can access product specification, and alternative and complementary items that then may be stored on a personal Web account.

The dressing rooms also contain a video-based 'magic mirror' that not only reveals the customer's back but also displays a delayed playback when the customers turns: a mirror that works in time as well as in space. In addition, multiple lighting scenarios allow the customer to change the atmosphere of the dressing room and consider choices in several light environments. Dressing room doors transform from translucent to transparent with a simple switch, to afford waiting companions a quick look.

When it is launched in January 2002, the Web presence will be the first phase of the service section of a larger Web site and is aimed at extending the relationships formed in the store into the virtual.

To maintain an exclusive and personal relationship, only products that have been tried in the store or recommended by a salesperson can be investigated on the Web site. Personalized customer care that is provided by sales associates in-store can continue on-line. In this way each store is its own small fulfillment and customer care center.

literature
OMA/OMA, Rem Koolhaas, Projects for Prada, part 1,
Milan 2001

Rem Koolhaas/OMA, *Prada New York, changing room,* 2001

Konstantin Grcic/Glas.com, Diana side table by BD/Es

Diana Side Tables 2002

Konstantin Grcic (1965)

Konstantin Grcic/Classicon, Diana side table F, 2002, enamelled bent sheet steel

The Munich-based designer Konstantin Grcic has designed a series of metal side tables that are cut by laser from a thick metal plate. A few folds make the two-dimensional jigsaw pieces into spatial pieces of furniture. The simplest of them do exactly what you would expect of a side table. They are generic. The more complex tables in the series have multifunctional extras such as a bookstand or a lectern.

You have designed the tables for Classicon …
I have worked together with Classicon for about ten years. In 2001 I designed the 'Chaos' chair for them. This chair is not so simple to read. I needed to add something else to the chair in order to make the idea behind the chair clearer. The chair must have a context, more explanation. So, the tables were conceived as the assistants for the chair. In the end the side tables have become an independent group.
The idea of making the tables from folded sheet metal came about because Classicon works with an interesting factory here in the environs of Munich. It wasn't about getting the most out of the production process. For me that has never been an aim in itself.

How did they come about?
We made the first model from cardboard. Life-size. I always work at 1:1. Only then do you see what you're doing; how the table relates to the chair and the space around it. With laser-cutting and bending you can do really exceptional things. The housing of all computers is made like that nowadays, and I think that is a really important and interesting fact. But I wanted to resist such complex structures, and instead to do exactly the opposite, to make something that is actually very simple. By using thick metal plate I was able to avoid a complicated construction. Then, just folding was enough. Such a table is quite heavy, but actually for this design weight isn't really a concern. To the eye, the tables remain more legible. Now you can easily see how they were made. I think that is a very beautiful point.

Simplification is a continuous strand in your work …
Yes, that's right. For me it is essentially about the simplification of the idea. For me the form is a less essential problem. I enjoy the form – that is fun to work with. And that is also often the simplest part of the process. The combining of form and fabrication – I never have difficulty with that. I always feel much more secure with that. That is a logic that I need to think about much less. The refinement of the idea is really the most difficult part.

Until now you have mainly designed 'simple' products such as furniture and house-hold accessories. Does it interest you to make complex technical appliances?
At the moment I am working for a manufacturer of electrical kitchen appliances. But actually I find it far more difficult to design a chair, to work on something in

I approached the design of the Diana tables as if I were a typographer. Just like the cut of a font character, the tables are the result of repeated, careful reworking. Each line, each radius, each surface was examined again and again for its proportion and form, and corrected accordingly. This type of work is not based on any system. The only corrective is my subjective eye, my intuition. The metaphor of the font character is also appropriate in the sense that the letters of the alphabet form a word only in conjunction with other letters. It is only in conjunction with other products and furniture that the tables reveal their intended purpose.

Grcic in *Domus*, 2002

Photograph of the studio during the design of the side tables

Photograph of the studio during the design of the side tables in relation to the *Chaos chair*

which the technology is invisible. That requires great precision; the journey towards the final result is long and difficult. The nicest compliment anyone can pay me is to say that the energy I have invested in the process is invisible – that everything looks very simple.

If you have to place yourself in a historical perspective, do you feel more kindred to a designer such as Rietveld or to someone such as Buckminster Fuller?
Rietveld or Buckminster Fuller? Do I have to choose? Rietveld is one of the designers that I discovered for myself a long time ago. When I was still young it was extremely interesting and clarifying to study his work. Rietveld was a craftsman, which means that his ideas were generated by elementary experience and a thorough understanding of materials.
I discovered Buckminster Fuller much later. Of course he is theoretically very important for his world view, for his vision of the future.

Your work is very often generic. How generic are your side tables?
There is certainly something generic about A and B. My work is often generic. That interests me enormously. I love the fact that things are self-evident. I like to surround myself with those sorts of things. Generic things are uncomplicated, clear and self-evident. I don't think that design should be difficult to understand. You should be able to see what is happening.

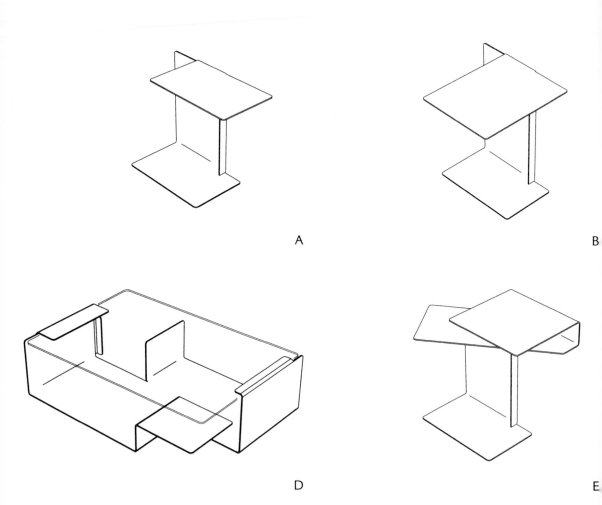

A

B

D

E

The series ranges from very simple and discreet (table A and B) to very large and complex (D). The final two even consist of two components (E and F) …

E and F were the first. They were the beginning of the design trajectory. For me it was very logical to make the complex ones first. In the beginning the idea is still complex. With me the process is always to simplify the idea, to distil it to its essentials. A and B were the last ones.

literature
F. Picchi, 'Changing Course, Konstantin Grcic', *Domus*, (847) April 2002, pp. 140-145

Konstantin Grcic/Classicon, *Diana side tables A–F*, 2002

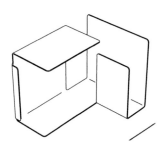

C

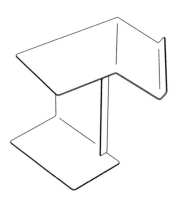

F

My way of thinking continues to be driven by logic; you analyse things and then you make the next logical decision.

Grcic in *Domus*, 2002

information
www.classicon.com
www.konstantingrcic.com

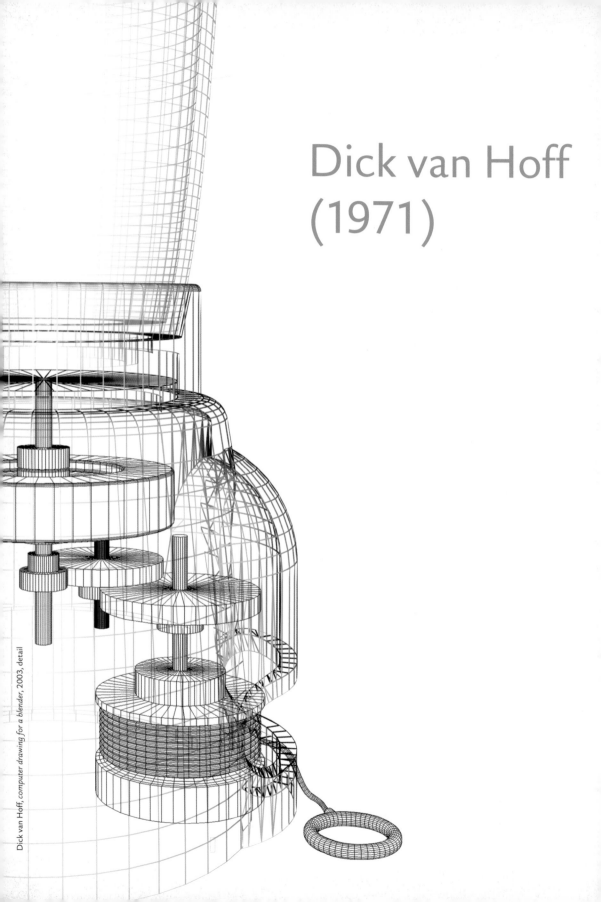

Dick van Hoff
(1971)

Prototypes
Kitchen Appliances
2003

Press Release, Milan 2003

BEYOND THE TYRANNY OF THE PLUG
Ingenious kitchen appliances by Dick van Hoff

A kitchen appliance that doesn't require a plug. A blender that continues to work even if there is a sudden power cut. Dick van Hoff designs appliances that are entirely tailored to the high quality expectations of the contemporary citizen, but which require more input than simply the use of the on/off switch. Technological progress has provided ingenious solutions to a great many problems. Still the doubt remains if all so-called progress is deserving of the term. We may not need to doubt the usefulness of a dishwasher, but why should we hand over the pleasures of cooking to machines that save us a mere minute or even seconds? And why should we make ourselves reliant on wall sockets or the availability of electricity for all activities? The minute it fails there is absolute panic. Dick van Hoff is also critical of the presumption that virtually all contemporary products are fitted with a plug, whilst no-one ever poses the question whether this offers the most pleasant and the most logical solution. For this reason he decided to design appliances that not only possess modern 'user-friendliness', but which also function under all circumstances.

Is Van Hoff denying modernity? Has he chosen for the nostalgic re-sue of old technologies and materials? Doe he strive for ecological purism at the cost of modern ease? Not at all. The world is awash with pseudo-handy solutions and hip status symbols, but the same world is once again becoming suspicious of the surfeit of useful, and above all not-so-useful products. The throw-away society is on its way back and the search for improvements in quality requires a critical consideration of options. Ecology certainly plays an important role in the choice of clever solutions, which do not harm the environment. But more important for Van Hoff is the simple question: why modern citizens make themselves reliant upon external energy supplies for activities that are worthwhile experiencing at first hand? His cooker, blender, mixer, ice cream maker and lemon press are made from cast iron, chrome, glass and wood and are made easy to use by such simple operations as winding up, pulling, spinning and moving back and forth.

Louise Schouwenberg

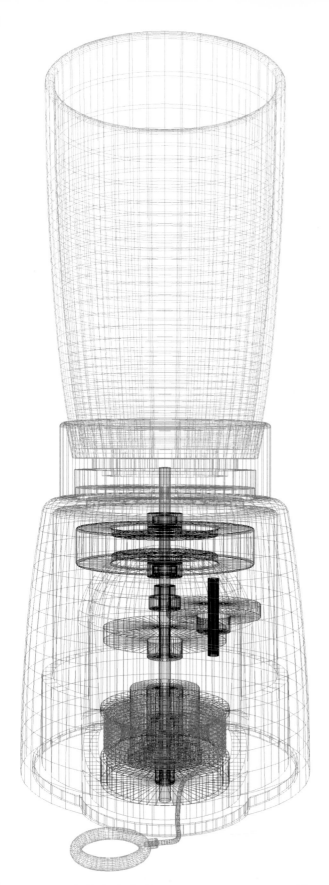

Amongst the generation of young Dutch designers who have created an international furore, Dick van Hoff is the inventor-constructor. His designs are always clear and without any frills. They are invariably based on generic types – they look and function as people expect them to. Nonetheless, in each case he has managed to improve the product, simplify its form and make it easier to use than its predecessor, which has served its purpose adequately for many years.

His tap, one of his graduation pieces at the Arnhem Institute for the Arts in 1995, is nothing more than the visual and physical combination of two copper water pipes, one for hot and the other for cold water. Where the two different sources are mixed, the pipes meet in a graceful arch. Two standard brass tap handles complete his design, making the user aware of their handling to determine the correct water temperature.

His concrete wood-burning stove from 2000 is derived from tiled stoves that have existed for centuries. Once the thermal mass of the concrete has been heated to a particular temperature, it gives off a pleasant heat for hours. The stove is Van Hoff's first design in which ecological factors play a central role.

The manually operated multifunction kitchen appliances, which respond to a request from

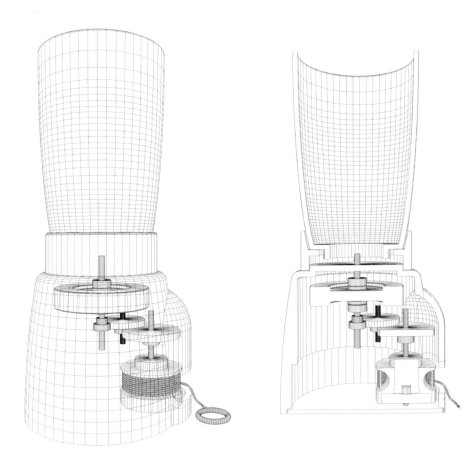

Museum Boijmans Van Beuningen as a reflection upon the selection made for *The Origin of Things*, show that many appliances that appear to save time, actually do not justify their existence in electronic versions. Who doesn't recall the electric carving knife, the electric can-opener and the electric knife-sharpener – the ultimate expressions of the modernised kitchen of the 1970s? They are now rightly regarded as exaggerations. Anyone who has used a professional hand-whisk to beat cream knows that it is a piece of cake; and to press half a lemon you can invariably choose a simple glass lemon press rather than an electrical one. But whether similar age-old kitchen aids have sufficient resistance to withstand the appeal of these whizzing and rattling appliances, resplendent with cogs and flywheels, remains to be seen.

The kitchen appliances were exhibited at the *Salon di mobile* in Milan from 9th-14th April 2003.

information
www.vanhoffontwerpen.nl

Authors

Philip van Daalen (1969)
is a historian, writer and lecturer. He has worked as a researcher
for the Stedelijk Museum in Amsterdam, the Centraal Museum
in Utrecht and the educational broadcaster Teleac. He was
also an advisor to the Art & Design Department of the Dutch
postal and telecommunications service (KPN) and since 2003
has lectured at the Design Academy in Eindhoven.

Thimo te Duits (1962)
is Curator of Twentieth-Century Design and Decorative Arts at
Museum Boijmans Van Beuningen. He has a specialist
knowledge of the Glasfabriek Leerdam. He has organised many
exhibitions at Museum Boijmans Van Beuningen including
Martin Margiela (1997) and *Walter van Beirendonck* (1998) in
collaboration with Marc Newson. He has contributed to
numerous publications in the fields of glass, ceramics, fashion
and industrial design.

Lesley Hoskins (1950)
is the Curator of the Museum of Domestic Design & Architecture at Middlesex University. She specialises in domestic
interiors of the nineteenth and twentieth centuries and has a
particular interest in wallpapers. She edited *The Papered Wall.
The History, Patterns and Techniques of Wallpaper* (1994). Her
other publications include *Living Rooms. 20th-Century Interiors*
(Geffrye Museum, 1998) and 'The Wallpapers of William
Morris' in *William Morris, 1834-1896* (1996).

Peter van Kester (1955)
is a historian of art and design. Following his graduation in 1984
he worked in the Amsterdam-based design gallery Binnen,
where he organised exhibitions about designers including
Konstantin Grcic, Michele de Lucchi, Ingo Maurer, Jasper
Morrison and Ettore Sottsass. He became a free-lance art
historian in 1999. He has written for many journals and
exhibition catalogues, curated exhibitions and coordinated art
commissions.

Henrik Most (1963)
is a lecturer in design at the University of Copenhagen and a
free-lance curator. He is currently engaged on a research project
entitled *Danish Design since 1980 – a Post-Structuralist Study.*
He published among other things *Vision and Reality in Twentieth
Century Design and Craft Art* and *Reliqvium* (both in 2002).

Paolo Palma (1973)
is a graphic and typographic designer. After collaborating for two years with the Dolcini Associati studio in Pesaro, he worked for Fabrica, the communication research center for the Benetton group. His work has been featured in numerous publications including *Colors, Domus, Linea Grafica, Modo, Novum* and *Print* and was the subject of the exhibition *Paradise. Image and type by Paolo Palma* (Bologna, 2001). His graduation thesis *New Alphabet. Wim Crouwel e la tipografia sperimentale* was published in book form in February 2003.

Jane Pavitt (1967)
is the Victoria & Albert Museum/University of Brighton Senior Research Fellow in Product Design and Museology. She has curated several exhibitions on contemporary design issues, including *Brand.New* (V&A, 2000) with Gareth Williams. She writes widely on design and design history. She is currently working on a book and exhibition about lighting, and leading the project to redisplay the twentieth-century galleries at the V&A.

Michael Siebenbrodt (1951)
is an architectural historian, writer and lecturer. Until 1985 he lectured in architectural history, theory and conservation at the Hochschule für Architektur und Bauwesen in Weimar. In 1979 and 1983 he managed the International Bauhaus Colloquium and from 1985 to 1988 he was the Director of the Bauhaus Museum and Bauhaus Theatre in Dessau. He has written and contributed to numerous publications on the Bauhaus and twentieth-century art, architecture and design.

Johan Soetens (1931)
was the Commercial Director of the Vereenigde Glasfabrieken (United Glassworks Schiedam-Leerdam-Maastricht) until 1996. He has organised numerous projects and exhibitions including the permanent display of historical bottle machines in Schiedam (1996), the glass blowing manifestation *Dare to be Square* and the exhibition *Het vierkant en de fles* in Leerdam (both in 2002). He wrote the standard work *Packaged in Glass. European Bottles, their History and Production* (2001).

Penny Sparke (1948)
is the Dean of the Faculty of Art, Design & Music and Professor of Design History at Kingston University in London. Since 1975 she has taught design history at Brighton Polytechnic and, from 1981 to 1999, at the Royal College of Art in London. Her numerous publications on design history include *An Introduction to Design and Culture in the Twentieth Century* (1986); *Italian Design from 1860 to the Present* (1989); *Japanese Design* (1989) and *As Long as it's Pink. The Sexual Politics of Taste* (1995).

Pauline Terreehorst (1952)
is the Director of the Amsterdam Fashion Institute, part of the Hogeschool van Amsterdam. She also teaches film theory at the University of Nijmegen. From 1985 to 2000 she was the fashion correspondent for Dutch daily newspaper *de Volkskrant*. She has published widely on visual culture and also acts as a consultant.

Gareth Williams (1966)
is a curator at the Victoria & Albert Museum, London, where he is currently preparing a new Architecture Gallery to open in 2004 in partnership with the Royal Institute of British Architects. He specialises in twentieth-century and contemporary furniture and product design, and has curated various exhibitions at the V&A including *Ron Arad Before and After Now* (with Sorrel Hershberg, 2000), *Brand.New* (with Jane Pavitt, 2000), *Milan in a Van* (2002) and *Matali Crasset. Unpacking Design* (2003). He has written and contributed to numerous books and journals including *Blueprint, Crafts, Design Week* and the *RIBA Journal*.

Peter Zwaal (1961)
is the historian and curator of the Nationaal Likeur- en Frisdrankenmuseum (National Liquor and Soft Drinks Museum) in Hilvarenbeek. He has published on a broad range of subjects and is currently working on a study of the Bavaria brewery in Lieshout.

Translator

Gerard Forde (1968)
is a free-lance translator, writer, curator and lecturer. He curated the exhibitions *Design in the Public Service – the Dutch PTT 1920-1990* (Design Museum, 1990) and *Paul Citroen and Erwin Blumenfeld 1919-1939* (Photographers' Gallery, 1993). He was a curator at the Design Museum from 1996-1999, where he curated exhibitions including *Ferdinand Porsche – Design Dynasty*. From 1999-2003 he was the resident writer and exhibitions organiser for the architectural practice Foster and Partners in London. He was the guest editor of *Emigre*'s special issue on Dutch design in 1993 and has written for *Beaux Arts, Eye, Domus* and *Jong Holland*.

Colophon

This publication accompanies the exhibition
The Origin of Things
10 May – 27 July 2003
at Museum Boijmans Van Beuningen, Rotterdam

This publication was made possible, in part,
by Fortis, Utrecht
and the Mondriaan Foundation, Amsterdam

Exhibition
Concept:
Thimo te Duits, Rotterdam
Design:
Wim Crouwel, Amsterdam

Publication
Concept:
Thimo te Duits, Rotterdam
Design:
Gracia Lebbink, Amsterdam

Text:
Philip van Daalen
(Rietveld, Loewy, Olivetti)
Thimo te Duits
(Cuypers, Colenbrander, Berlage, Wright, Gilles (with special
thanks to Emma Fitzgerald), Kho Liang Ie, Maison Martin
Margiela, Jongerius, Wanders, Koolhaas (ed.), Grcic, Van Hoff)
Lesley Hoskins
(Morris)
Peter van Kester
(Paperclip, Buckminster Fuller, Wirkkala, Mendini, De Lucchi,
Roelandt)
Henrik Most
(Henningsen, Panton)
Paolo Palma
(Crouwel)
Jane Pavitt
(Dyson)
Michael Siebenbrodt
(Bogler)
Johan Soetens
(Odol Bottle)
Penny Sparke
(Newson)
Pauline Terreehorst
(Galliano/Dior)
Gareth Williams
(Morrison)
Peter Zwaal
(Kiljan)

Copy editing:
Thimo te Duits, Rotterdam
Text editing:
Marianne Lahr, Diepenveen
Picture editing:
Thimo te Duits, Rotterdam; Gracia Lebbink, Amsterdam

Translation:
www.gerardforde.com, London;
Ishbel Flett, Edinburgh (Bogler D-E)

Typesetting and DTP:
Willem Morelis, Amsterdam

Printing and lithography:
Die Keure, Bruges

Production:
Brecht Bleeker, NAi Publishers, Rotterdam

Publisher:
NAi Publishers, Rotterdam with
Museum Boijmans Van Beuningen, Rotterdam

Photography

Museum Boijmans Van Beuningen, Rotterdam (NL)
Tom Haartsen
(unless mentioned otherwise)
Gerrit Schreurs
(cover, 4-6, 9 below, 32, 37, 184-185, 189)
Bob Goedewaagen
(74 left, 82)
Archive Gilles
(20-21, 109-110, 114-115, 126-130, 132-133)

and
ADAGP, Paris (F), *Willy Maywald* 218-219
Bauhaus Universität, Weimar (D) 51-55
Centraal Museum, Utrecht (NL) 88, 89 and 91
ClassiCon, Munich (D) 264, 265, 270 and 271
Allesandro Chiarato, Milan (I) 198-201
Christian Dior, Paris (F) 220-225
James Dyson, Malmesbury (GB) 202-205, 208-209
The Estate of Buckminster Fuller, Sebastopol CA (USA)
3 and 92-99
Frank Lloyd Wright Archive, Scottsdale AZ (USA) 81 right
and 83
Kasteel de Haar, Haarzuilens (NL) 45
Galerie Vivid, Rotterdam (NL) 156-157
Konstantin Grcic, Munich (D) 267-269
Groninger Museum, Groningen (NL) 180-182
Haags Gemeentemuseum, Den Haag (NL) 103 and
105-107
Dick van Hoff, Arnhem (NL) 272-275
JongeriusLab, Rotterdam (NL) 242-245
Kho Liang Ie Ass., Amsterdam (NL) 159-175
Friso Kramer, Amsterdam (NL), *Jan Versnel* 23 below
Kunstgewerbemuseum Staatliche Museen zu Berlin
Preußischer Kulturbesitz, Berlin (D) 48-49
Kunstindustrimuseet, Kopenhagen (DK) 122 and 123
Likeurmuseum Isodorus Jonkers, Hilvarenbeek (NL) 101,
102 and 104
Maison Martin Margiela, Paris (F), *Johannes Schweiger* 215;
Ronald Stoops 212-213; *Marina Faust* 211, 214 and 217
Jasper Morrison, Paris (F) 235-240
Museum Kröller Müller, Otterlo (NL) 1
Nationaal Glasmuseum Leerdam (NL), *Tom Haartsen* 75
right, 77 and 81 left
Nederlands Architectuur Instituut, Rotterdam (NL) 46, 47
and 69-73
Marc Newson, London (GB) 226-233
OMA, Rotterdam (NL) 253-263
Henri Petroski, Durham NY (USA) 33-39

Louis Poulsen, Kopenhagen (DK) 120 and 121
Johan Soetens, Rotterdam (NL) 43
Shell afbeeldingen (see Michael Johnson, *A Problem Solved. A
Primer in Design and Communication*, London 2002) 135-136
Stedelijk Museum, Amsterdam (NL) 86, 87 en 146-155
Taideteollisuusmuseo, Helsinki (Fin) 116-119
Victoria & Albert Museum, London (GB) 27 and 29
Vitra Design Museum, Weil am Rhein (D) 138-145
Marcel Wanders, Amsterdam (NL) 247 and 250-251
William Morris Society, Kelmscott House, London (GB) 24-25,
28 and 30

Lenders

Bauhaus Museum, Kunstsammlungen zu Weimar, Weimar (D)
Centraal Museum, Utrecht (NL)
Centro Studi Archivio della Comunicazione dell'Università di
Parma (CSAC), Parma (I)
Christian Dior, Paris (F)
ClassiCon, Munich (D)
Philip van Daalen, Rotterdam (NL)
DRU, Ulft (NL)
Dyson, Malmesbury (GB)
The Estate of Buckminster Fuller, Sebastopol, CA (USA)
Ford Motor Company, Detroit, MI (USA)
Frank Lloyd Wright Archive, Scottsdale, AZ (USA)
Gemeentearchief, Utrecht (NL)
Konstantin Grcic, Munich (D)
Haags Gemeentemuseum, Den Haag (NL)
Dick van Hoff, Arnhem (NL)
Kasteel de Haar, Haarzuilens (NL)
Kho Liang Ie Associates, Amsterdam (NL)
Kunstgewerbemuseum Staatliche Museen zu Berlin Preußischer
Kulturbesitz, Berlin (D)
Kunstindustrimuseet, Copenhagen (DK)
Likeurmuseum Isidorus Jonkers, Hilvarenbeek (NL)
Magis, Motta di Livenza (I)
Jasper Morrison, Paris (F)
Museum für Angewandte Kunst, Gera (D)
Museum voor Moderne Kunst, Arnhem (NL)
Nationaal Glasmuseum, Leerdam (NL)
Nederlands Architectuur Instituut, Rotterdam (NL)
OMA, Rotterdam (NL)
Stedelijk Museum, Amsterdam (NL)
Taideteollisuusmuseo, Helsinki (Fi)
Vitra Design Museum, Weil am Rhein (D)
Marcel Wanders, Amsterdam (NL)
Whitworth Art Gallery, Manchester (GB)
William Morris Society, Kelmscott House, London (GB)

Acknowledgements

Colleagues at Museum Boijmans Van Beuningen, Rotterdam
Project group *The Origin of Things*
Authors
Lenders

Special thanks to:

Marianne Aav, Taideteollisuusmuseo, Helsinki (Fin)
Juliette Allaire, Dyson, Paris (F)
Archivo Storico Olivetti, Ivrea (I)
Mario Bellini Associati S.r.l., Milan (I)
Allesandro Chiarato, I.E.D., Milan (I)
Wim Crouwel, Amsterdam (NL)
Luca Dosi Delfini, Stedelijk Museum, Amsterdam (NL)
James Dyson, Malmesbury (GB)
Titus Eliens, Haags Gemeentemuseum, Den Haag (NL)
Hellen Elletson, William Morris Society, London (GB)
Emily Ewing, Ford Motor Company, Detroit, MI (USA)
John Peter Ferry, The Estate of Buckminster Fuller, Sebastopol,
    CA (USA)
Emma Fitzgerald, Amsterdam (NL)
Gerard Forde, London (GB)
Penny Fowler, Frank Lloyd Wright Archive, Scottsdale, AZ (USA)
Wim Gilles†, Ontario (CA)
Caroline Glazenburg, Stedelijk Museum, Amsterdam (NL)
Pamela Golbin, Musée de la Mode, Louvre, Paris (F)
Konstantin Grcic, Munich (D)
Twan Haanen, Rotterdam (NL)
Frans Haks, Amsterdam (NL)
N. Hinse, Kasteel de Haar, Haarzuilen (NL)
Dick van Hoff, Arnhem (NL)
Hans-Peter Jakobson, Museum für Angewandte Kunst, Gera (D)
Hella Jongerius, Rotterdam (NL)
Eng Bo Kho, Amsterdam (NL)
Rem Koolhaas, OMA, Rotterdam (NL)
Aad Krol, Galerie Vivid, Rotterdam (NL)
Bodil Busk Laursen, Kunstindustrimuseet (DK)
Maison Martin Margiela, Paris (F)
Alfred Marks, NAi, Rotterdam (NL)
Hadewych Martens, Museum voor Moderne Kunst, Arnhem (NL)
Serge Maudit, Vitra Design Museum, Weil am Rhein (D)
Jasper Morrison, Paris (F)
Phillipe Le Moult, Christian Dior, Paris (F)
Marc Newson, London (GB)
Marianne Panton, Basel (CH)
Helen van Ruiten, Galerie Binnen, Amsterdam (NL)
Erna Onstenk, Haags Gemeentemuseum, Den Haag (NL)
Soizic Pfaff, Christian Dior, Paris (F)
Henry Petroski, Duke University, Durham, NY (USA)
A. Pietersma, Gemeentearchief Utrecht (NL)
David Quai, Amsterdam (NL)
Alice Rawsthorn, Design Museum, London (GB)
Aart Roelandt, Amsterdam (NL)
Ingeborg de Roode, Stedelijk Museum, Amsterdam (NL)
Gill Saunders, Victoria & Albert Museum, London (GB)
Ole Scheerer, OMA, Rotterdam (NL)
Michael Siebenbrodt, Bauhaus Museum, Weimar (D)
Petra Timmer, Amsterdam (NL)
Marcel Wanders, Amsterdam (NL)
Klaus Weber, Bauhaus-Archiv, Berlin (D)
Gareth Williams, Victoria & Albert Museum, London (GB)
Christine Woods, Whitworth Art Gallery, Manchester (GB)
Patsy Youngstein, Marc Newson, London (GB)
Ida van Zijl, Centraal Museum, Utrecht (NL)

Bijzondere Begunstigers

ABN AMRO
CALDIC
Imtech NV
DURA VERMEER GROEP N.V.
Aon Groep Nederland bv
Koninklijke Nedlloyd N.V.
Unilever
Loyens & Loeff
Koninklijke Econosto N.V.
Koninklijke Vopak N.V.
Fortis Bank
Ernst & Young
Nauta Dutilh
Siemens Nederland N.V.
Bakker Beheer Barendrecht BV
Nationale Nederlanden
Van der Vorm Vastgoed B.V.
GlaxoSmithKline B.V.
HAL Investments B.V.
KPMG Accountants Belastingadviseurs Consultants
Stichting Organisatie van Effectenhandelaren te Rotterdam
Nidera Handelscompagnie b.v.
Automobielbedrijf J. van Dijk & Dochters b.v.
KOEN VISSER GROEP
Stad Rotterdam Verzekeringen
Gebrs. Coster Beheer B.V.
Croon Elektrotechniek B.V.
Gemeente Rotterdam, Afdeling Externe Betrekkingen
De Brauw Blackstone Westbroek
Rendra

NAi Publishers is an internationally orientated publisher
specialised in developing, producing and distributing books on
architecture, visual arts and related disciplines.
www.naipublishers.nl info@naipublishers.nl

It was not possible to find all the copyright holders of the
illustrations used. Interested parties are requested to contact
NAi Publishers, Mauritsweg 23, 3012 JR Rotterdam,
The Netherlands.

Available in North, South and Central America through
D.A.P./Distributed Art Publishers Inc, 155 Sixth Avenue,
2nd Floor, New York, NY 10013-1507, Tel 212 627 1999,
Fax 212 627 9484.
Available in the United Kingdom and Ireland through Art Data
12 Bell Industrial Estate, 50 Cunnington Street, London W4
5HB, Tel 208 747 1061, Fax 208 742 2319.

Printed and bound in Belgium

ISBN 90-5662-318-4